DATE DUE

more to the story of human sexuality and relationships than the Viagra Myth would have us believe. The Viagra Myth has less to do with the effectiveness of the medication than with our cultural propensity to look for the easy fix. This myth suggests that a pill that improves blood flow to the penis can solve personal relationship issues, no matter how complex.

I started wondering about the disconnect between the Viagra Myth and reality soon after I had started prescribing the medication. John, a fifty-five-year-old man married for over twenty years, saw me three months after I had prescribed Viagra as treatment for his erectile dysfunction, with which he had suffered for over two years.

"So, John, how's the Viagra working out for you?" I asked.

"Well, it works, Doc. But I don't take it anymore."

"Why not?"

"To tell you the truth, my wife and I decided to separate. All this time, I'd thought that if I could have sex with her again, everything would work out fine. But it turns out that our problems are bigger than the sex thing. So we're splitting up."

Viagra had done wonders for John's erection problem but nothing toward solving his relationship problem.

Then there was Chester, who at seventy-one years old had initially complained that his erections were only semifirm. Sex with his wife had become awkward and unsatisfying, and he asked specifically for a prescription for Viagra. It seemed a reasonable request, and his physical exam revealed no health risks, so I prescribed the medication. When Chester returned to the office several months later, he reported on various other medical issues but never mentioned how he was doing sexually, even though that had been the main concern for him at his last visit.

"Did you ever try the Viagra?" I asked.

Chester gave me a big smile, and there was a gleam in his eye. "Oh, the Viagra! Well, it definitely makes me harder!" he chuckled. "But I don't need it. The wife and I are okay with how things are going without it. I don't want to spoil her, you know!"

Former senator and presidential candidate Bob Dole appeared in Pfizer ads soon after Viagra's introduction and instantly turned into household words the terms *Viagra* and *ED*. Viagra jokes became a staple of comedy acts on late-night television (Have you heard the one about the man who swallowed Viagra, but it stuck in his throat? He wound up with a very stiff neck!), thus ensuring its place in our cultural lexicon. Viagra tapped into both our fantasies and our embarrassment about sexuality in a way that no other drug had ever done. When, for example, was the last time you heard a joke about a new cholesterol-lowering medication?

Skillful marketing contributed to our perception of Viagra as the pill that put the "man" in "manly." Star professional athletes— vigorous men such as baseball's Most Valuable Player Rafael Palmeiro of the Texas Rangers and NASCAR driver Mark Martin—endorse the medication in widely seen advertisements. Other kinds of athletes use Viagra as well. Hugh Hefner, the aging head of the Playboy empire who is known for his bevy of beautiful blondes, gives Viagra credit for maintaining his pleasure quotient. Rumor has it that he provides bowls of Viagra tablets at his famous parties.

Magical Viagra. A wonder drug. Or so we have come to believe. But does the reality live up to the myth? Is it really *that* good? Can it truly solve erection problems? What about relation-ship issues? What does Viagra do for a man who has lost his sexual desire or for a man who is simply nervous about having sex with a new partner? What's the real story?

As someone who treats men with Viagra nearly every day, I can tes-tify to the remarkable effects of this medication. For many men and their partners, Viagra has unquestionably brought about significant improvements in their lives, and to a degree that was not previ-ously possible with other treatments. And yet there is clearly much me in the surgeons' lounge as I was having a cup of coffee between operations.

"Tell me," he said, "what should I know about prescribing Viagra? I have a patient who I think should try it."

Now I have great respect for my orthopedic colleagues, but I have yet to meet one who would take on the treatment of a problem outside his area of expertise in bones and cartilage. It was quite clear that this surgeon's patient was none other than himself!

Everyone wants to know about Viagra, and many are interested in trying it, whether or not they think they have an erection problem. When I lecture to students at Harvard Medical School about sexuality, there are always a good number of Viagra questions, such as, "What happens when a young, healthy man with normal sexual function takes Viagra?" Or "Can a woman tell during sex that her partner has taken Viagra?" Or "Is it true that Viagra increases a man's sex drive?" No one ever falls asleep in those classes!

Viagra quickly tapped into a set of wishful fantasies that mirrored our culture's hunger for certainty and the quick fix. Supported by stories that described elderly men restored to such sexual vitality by Viagra that they abandoned their wives in favor of younger women, a conventional wisdom arose that Viagra was a fountain of youth, a sure cure, the real deal. Baby boomers could now look forward to fabulous sex well into their nineties. Men shared Viagra stories with each other at cocktail parties or around the office water cooler.

"All I can say is 'Wow!'" says one man, and other men listening in wonder how their lives might be different if they also took the magic blue pill.

Women too have been targeted to confirm Viagra's ability to create satisfaction and serenity within a relationship where frustration and friction had once been the rule. One of the most successful early Pfizer ads showed a series of couples happily dancing together after Viagra apparently cured the loss of rhythm in their relationship.

Introduction

In 1998, Viagra was first introduced to the world, and it is fair to say that the world has not been the same since. The impact of this medication has been enormous, not just in the narrow area of treating erectile dysfunction (ED) for which it was approved, but also in the way we think of sex and sexuality, and even in the realm of relationships between men and women.

Millions of men in the United States have tried Pfizer's wonder drug, sildenafil, better known as Viagra, and there are thus millions of women who have also seen its effects on their husbands, boyfriends, and lovers. Many other millions of men and women wonder about whether Viagra can offer a solution for their own sexual and emotional problems or for the problems of their partners. We human beings are sexual animals, after all. And unfortunately, our sex lives are not always the way we want them to be. So it's no surprise that when sex goes sour, relationships suffer in other ways as well.

As a practicing urologist in Boston on the faculty of Harvard Medical School, I have treated many men with sexual problems and many couples who have sexual issues in their relationships. I knew about the development of Viagra before it was introduced to the public and was involved in its clinical application as soon as the Food and Drug Administration approved the new drug. I had anticipated using Viagra primarily for older patients with well-established erectile dysfunction, but it didn't take long before I realized that I had completely underestimated the huge extent of public interest in trying this new medication. For example, shortly after Viagra became available, an orthopedic surgeon came up to

The Viagra Myth

acquaintances with whom I discussed various aspects of the book and who provided me with some of the vignettes that I have shamelessly borrowed and included here.

As always, my staff at Men's Health Boston took care of all the details of my practice while I directed my attention to the completion of this book. I am so proud of Kerry and Randy Eaton, Kevin Flinn, Stephanie Hayes, Vicki Zdanovich, and Mel Delger for creating the warmest and most professional medical environment in Boston.

Finally, I give thanks to my patients, the men and women who find the courage to share their stories and struggles with me. I hope this book does justice to their inspiring acts of bravery and honesty that I witness every day. Allowing me to contribute to their lives is a gift they give to me and has convinced me that I have the best job in the whole world.

Abraham Morgentaler, M.D., F.A.C.S.
Brookline, Massachusetts

Acknowledgments

This book evolved through various stages, and I would like to acknowledge Dr. Harold Burzstajn for recognizing the value of a book on the topic of Viagra and sexuality and suggesting the topic to me. Pat Wright and Dr. Laura Berman were part of our original "think tank" regarding a book on Viagra and were instrumental in moving the project forward from concept to concrete proposal. Pat introduced me to my agent, Jim Levine, who provided the insightful criticism that made the project focused and worthy of finding a publisher. Pat also did an excellent job writing an engaging book proposal.

It has been my great fortune to become connected with my editor, Alan Rinzler, at Jossey-Bass. How wonderful to have someone understand what I want to say and then help me find the words to express it clearly. Alan's wisdom, keen ear, and sure hand shaped this book into a coherent whole. Thank you, Alan. I give thanks also to Jennifer Wenzel, Ellen Silberman, and Gary Stromberg for marketing and publicity, and to Carol Hartland for production management and Bev Miller for copyediting.

I am blessed to have been born into a family of writers. My father, Dr. Henry Morgentaler, read every word of the manuscript and provided valuable suggestions and criticisms. My mother, Chawa Rosenfarb, and my sister, Dr. Goldie Morgentaler, read selected chapters and gave me encouragement and support. Dear friends Mike Schopperle and Bonnie St. John read portions of the manuscript for me. Thanks, too, to the other wonderful friends and

*To my sister, Goldie, for her unwavering love, and to my children,
Maya and Hannah, for bringing so much joy to my life*

Contents

Published by Jossey-Bass
A Wiley Imprint
989 Market Street, San Francisco, CA 94103-1741   www.josseybass.com

Jossey-Bass books and products are available through most bookstores. To contact Jossey-Bass
directly call our Customer Care Department within the U.S. at 800-956-7739, outside the
U.S. at 317-572-3986, or fax 317-572-4002.

Jossey-Bass also publishes its books in a variety of electronic formats. Some content that
appears in print may not be available in electronic books.

The contents of this work are intended to further general scientific and medical understanding
and discussion only and are not intended and should not be relied upon as recommending or
promoting a specific method, diagnosis, or treatment for any particular situation. This work is
sold with the understanding that the publisher is not engaged in rendering medical or other
professional services. Before taking any drugs, the reader should always consult a physician.
The publisher and the author make no representations or warranties with respect to the
accuracy or completeness of the contents of this work and specifically disclaim all warranties,
including without limitation any implied warranties of fitness for a particular purpose. No
warranty may be created or extended by any promotional statements for this work. Neither
the publisher nor the author shall be liable for any damages arising herefrom. All names and
identifying characteristics of patients used in the case studies have been changed.

This book has not been prepared, approved, licensed, or endorsed by Pfizer, Inc., the owner of
the registered trademark "Viagra."

Library of Congress Cataloging-in-Publication Data
Morgentaler, Abraham.
   The Viagra myth : the surprising impact on love and relationships /
Abraham Morgentaler.
      p. cm.
Includes bibliographical references.
   ISBN 0-7879-6801-3
1. Sildenafil—Popular works. 2. Impotence—Popular works. I. Title.

RC889.M7585 2003
   616.6'92061—dc21
                                        2003006249

Printed in the United States of America
FIRST EDITION
HB Printing   10 9 8 7 6 5 4 3 2 1

The Viagra Myth

The Surprising Impact on Love and Relationships

JOSSEY-BASS
A Wiley Imprint
www.josseybass.com

Abraham Morgentaler, M.D., F.A.C.S.

The Viagra Myth

John and Chester are just two examples of the many men for whom Viagra works in a physical sense as it is supposed to, but the medication failed to meet their expectations in other ways. Even when Viagra works, men like John and Chester often do not want to take it, and their reasons vary. Although I saw these men in my practice every day and intently followed their stories, I was still surprised to learn that the refill rate for Viagra prescriptions is less than 50 percent. What happened to the old crude joke that all a man needs in order to be happy is a hard penis and a place to put it? Could our perception of Viagra and our sense of masculine sexuality be so out of kilter with reality?

Surprisingly the answer is yes. The Viagra Myth, which promotes the notion of the hard penis as the salvation of sexual relationships, is so pervasive that even professionals in the field bought into it. After reflecting on cases like those of John and Chester and their partners, I began to see an enormous gulf between appearances and reality when sexual relationships are in question.

Many of my male patients, together with many of their partners, came to realize that finally achieving a great erection did not solve their relationship problems. In fact, it frequently made them worse. As with John and his wife, sometimes when the erection issue is solved, couples are forced to deal with more profound troubles in the relationship.

As I listened to my patients, I came to see that our culture had taken Viagra and created a legend out of it that went far beyond its actual pharmacological properties. People had come to expect that taking a little blue pill could solve their personal and relationship problems, no matter how complex those difficulties were. I heard variations on this theme almost daily. Men or their partners requested prescriptions for Viagra for all sorts of problems, sometimes with the barest of sexual symptoms: a lack of desire, struggles in existing relationships, fear of intimacy, or a desire to be a sexual superstud, for example. The range of issues for which men could envision successful treatment only with Viagra was astounding to me. This aura surrounding a medication that enhances blood flow to the penis is clearly a reflection of who we are and our desire for the easy, quick fix. I have called this exaggerated sense of Viagra as a wonder drug for various complex issues the Viagra Myth.

Yes, the drug is enormously powerful, and it can be a lifesaver for many men, but it has also turned a bright spotlight on previously hidden areas of sexuality and relationships. In particular, it forces couples to decide what is real in their relationships and what is not. I have come to see Viagra as providing a window into the psyche of men, and perhaps indirectly into the psyche of women as well, since women are not immune from unduly high expectations regarding the benefits of Viagra and its potential to provide sexual healing.

The lessons I have learned by listening to my patients and their partners form the basis of this book, and in the pages that follow I share the stories of those who have taught me so much about sex and sexuality and, by extension, about personal growth and humanity.

The lessons to be learned are startling, profound, and often inspiring. What does it mean for a man to lose his sense of masculinity and self-esteem? How does this loss manifest itself in the relationship between him and his partner? How do couples survive when a man loses the ability to function sexually? What is it like when his sexual powers return? What is it like for a woman to have her partner restored to his "youthful vigor" after a prolonged period of inactivity?

This is a book about real people. The men and women who pass through my office share intimate details of their lives that would otherwise never see the light of day were it not for this book. Naturally, names and details have been changed in order to preserve privacy, and in many stories I have combined features from two or more patients. Each story is unique, yet there are themes familiar to every reader because of the commonality of human experience. Men want to feel powerful and capable and accepted, to be able to relate to their partners in a way that affirms these qualities. Women want to feel attractive to their partners and emotionally connected. When sex goes awry, particularly because of erection problems, not only do relationships come crashing down, but men and women lose their grip on these most fundamental human needs: secure identity and intimate connection.

To be sure, the power of Viagra lies in its ability to correct a man's erection problems. Whether this fix rights the ship depends on the individuals involved and what they bring of themselves on board. So often, as the stories that follow show, men and women are at cross-purposes within their relationships and lack a shared language for understanding each other. As we are continually reminded by advertisements and testimonials in the media, Viagra can help correct the erection problem. But if a man is worried only about his lost machismo while his partner is concerned about a lack of emotional intimacy, then the reappearance of a firm penis is not likely to provide them with a happily-ever-after. Both will fall victim to the Viagra Myth.

To dispel this myth and help readers distinguish between fact and fiction, this book seeks to answer some of the questions most frequently raised by my patients and their partners, such as the following:

- When is Viagra the "perfect" cure?
- When is Viagra not a cure but an obstacle to a relationship?
- How does a man determine whether his partner loves him or Viagra?
- What does a woman experience when she's with a man who can function sexually only with Viagra?
- If a man can function only with Viagra, does he continue to think of himself as impotent or does he feel inauthentic?
- Does Viagra make a man more virile, more attractive, and a better lover?
- What happens when a man doesn't tell his partner he's taking Viagra? Will she know? Is it the same as lying?

- What's the relationship between an erection and desire?
- Can Viagra work after prostate cancer surgery?
- If Viagra doesn't work for a man, will he ever be able to have sex again?
- Can a couple have sex without an erection?
- Does Viagra make sex less spontaneous and more predictable?

I have written this book in the hope of provoking a more thoughtful and frank discussion about sexuality than currently exists. On a practical level, I hope that men and women can use these stories as starting points to improve the dialogue they have with each other in their relationships and ultimately to create a more fully satisfying life for themselves. I also hope this book will lead to the more realistic application of Viagra and other sexual therapies for the benefit of all men, women, and their relationships.

Chapter One

Viagra and the Perfect Cure

Viagra is a recent invention, but sex is not. And for as long as humans have engaged in sexual activity, there has been impotence. The word *impotence* first appeared in the fifteenth century, but today it has been abandoned in politically correct circles in favor of the term *erectile dysfunction*, or more colloquially, ED.

Incredibly, it took a panel of experts to meet and decide on the name change. In 1993, at the Consensus Meeting of the National Institutes of Health, participants agreed that the failure of the penis to achieve and sustain adequate rigidity for sexual intercourse was equivalent to other types of organ failures, such as hepatic dysfunction for liver disease. Moreover, the experts recognized that the word *impotence* had negative connotations that should not be invoked just because a man's penis did not work properly. To be impotent, after all, means that someone lacks power, force, or effectiveness. Since we would not attribute such qualities to someone whose liver did not work well, the meeting attendees agreed that the term *impotence* should not be applied to men with erectile dysfunction.

Nevertheless, unlike men with liver disease, kidney disease, or rhythm disturbances of the heart, men with erectile dysfunction *do* in fact feel impotent, in the full sense of the word. For this reason, I continue to use the word interchangeably with erectile dysfunction. Depression, embarrassment, a diminished sense of masculinity—these are some of the feelings men experience when erectile dysfunction occurs.

Women are often surprised at the depth of despair men exhibit when the erection fails. Of course, it can be disappointing at the moment for both partners. But when it first happens to a couple, many women describe an "oh, well" attitude about it, with the expectation that there will be other opportunities later.

Only rarely do men have such a response. Typically, they experience a frenzy of anxiety and despair when they go soft during a sexual encounter. The experience is mocked in the first of the *Austin Powers* movies, when the comic sleuth Austin temporarily loses his "mojo." The cocky, sexually aggressive aspect of his persona disappears until he gets it back. On a much more serious note, many a young man fantasizes about being a great lover—a Casanova or Don Juan—but if his penis will not cooperate enough even to get started, then what hope of sexual greatness can he entertain? A torrent of questions rushes in on him when he experiences erectile dysfunction for the first time:

"What is happening?"

"Why?"

"Why now?"

"Does this mean that my penis is broken for good?"

"Will I never be able to have sex again?"

"Will she laugh at me?"

"Will she leave me?"

"Will she tell everyone and shame me?"

Since a normal erection occurs as if by magic, the failure of the penis to respond appropriately in a sexual situation can be an unpleasant mystery for the affected man. An erection is one of the few things in life that is not improved by greater determination and willpower. A woman may roll over and say nonchalantly, "Let's just sleep on it, and I bet things will be great in the morning." The man will probably not sleep a wink.

The following morning, he may try again, with enthusiasm of sorts, but instead of enjoying the moment, he is busy wondering, "Will it work? Is it hard enough?" His anxiety makes things worse. And if the second round and third round are also failures, the man is likely to enter into a deep funk from which it may be difficult to escape. He may want to give up on sex altogether and withdraw into his cave.

Men have a tendency to think in dramatic, action-oriented terms and absolutes such as, "I won't ever touch her again." But if a man then pulls away emotionally or physically, the woman may wonder if the lack of connection is *her* fault somehow: something she said, something she did. Women feel frustrated when things feel wrong and the man will not talk about it at all. The failure of the penis to respond can thus create enormous havoc in a relationship because of the different ways that men and women respond to sexual behavior and its less-than-clear messages.

The difference in sexual attitudes between men and women comes as no surprise to anyone who has spent more than a few years on this planet. Men and women differ in their attitudes toward so many things that it is sometimes hard to understand how they can enter into relationships with each other in the first place. When sex becomes a problem, those differences become magnified, and even long-standing relationships can suffer tremendously. How do the two people in a relationship regain their mojo?

Enter Viagra, complete with all its trappings and promises. The Viagra Myth sends a powerful message, claiming that the drug can restore a man to his full potency and rescue a relationship on the rocks. But how much truth is there in the Viagra ad that shows the satisfied husband whistling as he leaves for work the morning after popping the little blue pill, while his wife smiles as mysteriously as Mona Lisa while she sits at the breakfast table sipping her coffee, wrapped in her terrycloth robe? Is this nothing more than a fictitious, unrealistic advertising moment?

In truth, such moments do occur, and not infrequently. Viagra has changed the landscape of relationships, smoothing out some of the most difficult dips and valleys.

In order to understand the limits of the Viagra Myth, therefore, it is first necessary to see what happens when everything does go right. The ability of Viagra to bridge seemingly insurmountable relationship hurdles can be astounding, as demonstrated by the story that follows.

A Marriage in Trouble

One October day, George, a fifty-eight-year-old contractor, and his wife, Marie, arrived for their eleven o'clock appointment at my clinic, Men's Health Boston. George and Marie had driven from their home in Lynn, Massachusetts, a community northeast of Boston, where they had lived for some twenty-five years. Standing six feet three inches tall and weighing well over 250 pounds, George occupied practically every inch of the doorway as he entered the office. His wife, Marie, petite and fragile and a few years younger than George, seemed overshadowed by his huge presence, but she had a definite sense of determination about her. George seemed far less eager to be there.

Even without glancing at the chart, I knew why this couple had come to see me.

Despite all the publicity and frank talk we now hear about sex and erection problems on television talk shows and advertisements, only about 20 percent of men with erectile dysfunction problems ever seek professional help. When you consider that there are over 30 million men in the United States alone who experience some symptoms of erectile dysfunction, that means a large percentage of them continue to live with the diminished self-esteem and unhappiness that this problem creates.

The primary reason men do not seek help is shame. They are ashamed that they are impotent. They are ashamed that they cannot perform sexually as they once did or as they think they should. To make matters worse, there still exists the belief, left over from the work of human sexuality gurus Virginia Masters and William Johnson from the 1970s, that erection problems are most often psychological in nature. We now know that is not the case.

For many men, this assumption that their problem is psychological creates further confusion: "My erection problem is all in my head, and the solution is for me to get my head together in order to make this problem go away." Persistent failure then becomes a sign (in their own minds) of failed willpower in addition to a failed erection—another sign of a diminished masculinity.

Men often find it hard to come to the doctor's office in the first place. It is all the harder when the problem is sexual and the man perceives himself as less of a man. George's manner was typical of so many other men urged by their partners to visit the clinic. Reluctant sighs, arms crossed over chest, legs rhythmically bouncing up and down—I see it all the time. Curiously, for many of these men, this gruffness is all a show for the woman. I see much less of it when the man arrives alone for his appointment.

"He Never Touches Me Anymore"

"How can I help you?" I asked, inviting them both to sit down. George first settled Marie into one chair, then took the other one for himself. He looked at Marie in a way that communicated he was doing this only to humor her, then turned to me, and was silent for a moment.

"It just don't work anymore," George said finally, shrugging his shoulders.

"What do you mean?" I asked.

"It just doesn't get up," he answered.

George spoke in a way that betrayed his conviction, probably unconscious, that this problem was irreparable. He acted as if it were a giant waste of time for us to be sitting there together talking about this uncomfortable topic. None of us, of course, had any doubt as to what George meant by "it": we all knew that he was referring to an unresponsive penis, the one part of his physical being that, seemingly with a mind all its own, refused to get hard or stay that way.

"When did you notice the penis wasn't working properly?" I asked him, picking up on his metaphor of the body as some vast machine. Specifically referring to the "penis" had the advantage of cutting through a lot of euphemisms and providing clarity. Patients usually accept this forthrightness right away, using the words I use as if they have learned a new code. One of the great difficulties for many couples when talking about sex is that they don't really have a language to use together. Of course, both George and Marie knew the word *penis*, but it seemed highly unlikely that either one of them used the term with each other. This part of our societal sexual awkwardness makes it particularly challenging to deal with sexual issues when a problem arises.

"Well, uh, maybe a year or so ago," George said.

"It's been much longer than that, George," Marie corrected. "It started just after Elizabeth, our youngest child, left home to go to college. And I know that was in September a full two years ago. We've been married for over twenty-five years. For all those years, we hardly ever missed a Saturday night to have—well, you know— our special time together. We might put it off if one of us was not feeling good or one of the children was home for the weekend, but it was generally something we always counted on. In the last two years, however, we've not had a single Saturday night together. I mean, we're both there in the same bedroom, but, well, nothing happens."

George seemed visibly uncomfortable with Marie's revelation, especially to me, a complete stranger. Although George himself had told me that his penis no longer became firm enough for sex, Marie's description of her disappointment with George was even more damning. He clearly experienced this as her indictment of him as a husband.

"And it's not just in the bedroom," Marie continued, unaware of her husband's discomfort. "For the past two years, he hasn't touched me at all. It's gotten to the point where if we go to a movie, for example, and I reach over to hold his hand, he lifts my hand up and drops it back in my lap like an old dirty dishcloth."

George stared down at the sausages of his fingers folded together across the broad expanse of his stomach. With a thumbnail, he pried at the cuticle on the opposite thumb and kneaded his discomfort deeper into the loaf of his belly. His hands did the talking for him, expressing profound embarrassment at having been suddenly exposed as a less-than-powerful man who could no longer provide for his wife. He was, by all the signs of his physical and psychological makeup, a man of deeds, not words—a man who was used to shouldering responsibility and making sure that his wife was taken care of.

Nobody Is Happy

"George has always provided a good home for me and the children," Marie said. "He managed so that I never had to go to work, unlike his mother, who had to work two, sometimes three jobs to help support the family. He's been a good husband to me and a wonderful father to our three children. But since Elizabeth left for school, he hasn't been the same. Up until a few months ago, in fact, I actually thought he was having an affair because he seemed no longer interested in having . . . well, you know . . . a relationship with me."

"You know that's baloney," George said.

"So, let me understand this correctly. You mean that you haven't had sexual intercourse together for the past two years?" I asked.

"That's right," Marie said. "Deep down, I keep wondering if he's just no longer attracted to me."

"That's not true," George interrupted. "I've told you that a hundred times."

"That's what you say, but it's not what it looks like," Marie said, her voice quivering. "You stay up watching late-night TV and you think I'm asleep when you come to bed. But I know when you come in, and we've been married long enough so that I know when something's bothering you."

I waited, but neither one was ready to say more. "George, is there anything you'd like to say?" I encouraged.

"Doctor, Marie should really know better than to say some of those things. She knows I love her and that I'm not interested in anyone else." He paused. "The real reason I don't touch her is that I don't want her to get her hopes up, because I know I'm going to disappoint her if she does." There was a catch in his voice. "You know, I'm not happy about any of this."

"I Don't Feel Pretty Anymore"

George was clearly more comfortable with facts than he was with emotions. The very picture of good health, he took great pride in his physical condition, announcing that I was the first doctor he had seen in fifteen years. When he was in his early forties, the construction company he worked for had required him to get a physical exam in order to qualify for strenuous work on a contract with the city of Boston: he had passed with flying colors and saw no need to go back to a physician, not when he was feeling like a million bucks. Oh, he had the usual aches and pains, like the time he had pulled a muscle in his back when he tried to lift a steel plate single-handedly. But such injuries, he said, were common in his line of work. When he felt as good as he did, why did he need to see a doctor?

On the downside, he said, he didn't have the stamina he once had. He had first attributed the problem with sex to long hours at his job as a contractor and to the fact that he was, after all, getting on in years. His old engine had lost its kick, he told me. What he would give for a new or rebuilt model!

"So what happens when you try to have sex?" I asked, getting to the point that had brought them here. I learned long ago not to ask fuzzy questions such as, "How's your sex life?" Such queries either shut the door when patients respond only with, "It's fine," or open the floodgates to an assortment of details that may never get to the key issues. I prefer to ask fairly direct questions that provide me with information about what is occurring or not occurring when my patients engage in sexual activity.

"Well, like I said, it just don't work anymore."

"Do you mean the penis doesn't get hard?" I asked.

"That's right," he mumbled.

"Do you ever have an erection during the night or when you awaken in the morning?"

"I used to wake up in the morning with an erection, but that hasn't happened in a long, long time. I've even tried to work it myself, you know, just to see if I could get it to come up, but it won't work that way either."

George's story, told in few words, pointed to something physical, not psychological, at the root of his problem. Most commonly, this means that the blood vessels of the penis are not working properly, either by not supplying enough blood to the chambers in the penis or by letting the blood leave before it should, like a tire with an air leak. Either way—supply problem or leak problem—the penis remains soft even though the man may be completely aroused. Surprisingly, many men with a physical cause of erectile dysfunction often have normal sexual desire and can usually still ejaculate—have an orgasm and emit fluid—even though the penis is soft. It doesn't always happen that way, as we'll see later in this book, but a lot of my patients and their partners are amazed to hear that this can occur.

If the erectile dysfunction is psychological in nature, then there probably is nothing blocking the normal flow of blood to the penis except some deep anxiety. Thus, men with psychological reasons for their erectile dysfunction can usually achieve an erection with masturbation, or they will occasionally awaken from sleep with a firm penis. In reporting that he had not experienced an erection during sleep, George was letting me know that his problem was unlikely to be a psychological one. That said, it was abundantly clear that George had a psychological *response* to this problem that had affected his relationship with Marie to its core.

George's anxieties over his inability to achieve an erection had caused him to sever physical contact with Marie. He had stopped being affectionate. Indeed, he had retreated within the relationship and seemed to Marie withdrawn, possibly even depressed. He was in fact trying to protect himself from the pain of his failed masculinity, even though he thought he was protecting Marie from disappointment. She, in turn, was reading into his actions a rejection of her and her needs. She was afraid she was doing something wrong with George at every turn. No matter what she tried, he never seemed to respond to her anymore with his kind smile or the good-natured teasing that had been part of their relationship from the very start.

As George recounted his medical history and his problem, I glanced over at Marie. She looked tired and worn out, hungry for support and affirmation, neither of which she was getting from George. Dwarfed by his physical presence, she seemed defensive and vulnerable.

"I feel like there's something I should be doing to help him," Marie said after George finished his story. "I try to keep the house neat and hold the line on our expenses, but that doesn't seem enough. The worst of it is that lately, I don't feel pretty anymore."

Stunned, George looked at Marie, then quickly cast his eyes toward the floor. I had the sense that for the first time, George had seen the effect of his behavior on Marie.

The differences in the way the two people in this relationship saw the problem could not have been more evident. Marie told the story plaintively, as if she had lost something vitally important to her. She was looking to repair her relationship with George. He was hoping to repair his plumbing.

The Doctor's Dilemma

These differences in perspective between men and women create a dilemma for me. In this case, should I treat the male plumbing as a structural problem and hope that the relationship issues will take care of themselves? Or should I counsel the couple so that George can begin to see how his behavior has affected Marie beyond the loss of their lovemaking, and so that Marie can better understand George's feelings of sadness and inadequacy?

Every situation needs its own solution and balanced approach depending on the people involved and the sense of the relationship they provide. Many men are completely shut off from feelings and are quick to dismiss any discussion that feels "mushy" to them. Women, in contrast, often have difficulty grasping the concept of machismo and what it means to a man.

George and Marie's visit to the clinic represented an act of courage, perhaps with some desperation thrown in. It must have taken an enormous effort on Marie's part to challenge George to seek professional help for this problem that affected them both. In fact, many of the men I see begin their sessions by denying that they have any problem at all: "Oh, I sometimes can't get it up when I've had too much to drink," or "Sex really doesn't mean that much to me anymore, not since I turned fifty," or "You know the wife: she's already gone through menopause, and she says she's not much interested in sex." I hear excuses like these every day and understand them for what they are: attempts to lay blame at the door of alcohol, the aging process, or the inevitable changes of life.

Men are culturally trained to minimize problems. Beginning in grade school, boys are teased by other boys for going to the nurse for anything less than obvious broken bones or major lacerations. Even then, there is apparent virtue in toughing it out. Schoolyard names such as "Sissy" or "Momma's Boy" create a learning experience that is difficult to shake as men grow up and eventually require medical care. It is simply incongruous to imagine Arnold Schwarzenegger, Bruce Willis, or some other male action hero sitting down with his doctor to discuss his feelings or express concern about his sexual performance.

Women have a different relationship with the medical system. Many begin having regular doctor appointments during adolescence and rely on physicians for a range of issues in their lives that stretch far beyond the confines of what one usually considers medicine. Mothers, for example, routinely ask for advice from pediatricians on social issues such as bullying of their children at school or how to deal with sibling rivalry. Gynecologists are not surprised when patients bring up sexual concerns, discuss postpartum blues, or inquire about ways to spice up a long-term relationship that has gone stale. But for men, speaking to doctors about such issues, which they view as soft, is an entirely foreign concept.

"George," I said, "I'm glad that you came in to talk to me. I know it's a hard thing to do. Now, we can get down to the business of helping you out."

Getting over the Hump

George's medical history was unremarkable, and his physical examination gave no hint of any abnormalities that would contribute to his erectile dysfunction. I discussed the need for some diagnostic tests, and he nodded as if he understood my words, but reserved the right to decide whether to proceed after he had time to think it over. At the end of this first visit, I told George and Marie that I thought there was an excellent chance I could help them.

"That would be great, Doc," George said as he left the room, but it was clear he was not expecting much. This was a man who would not let himself be fooled by mere talk. Marie, in contrast, had brightened up considerably by the end of the visit. Her challenge now was to keep George on track with his tests and his next visit with me.

Viagra to the Rescue

George completed his tests and came back to see me, accompanied again by Marie. He had undergone a sleep test at home in which he was instructed to place two small rings around his penis before he went to sleep. In the morning, he removed them. The device functions as a miniature blood pressure recording unit. When plugged into our computer in the office, it provides a printout of the quality and duration of any erections that occur during sleep.

Since a man's excessive worrying about whether his penis is hard enough usually makes it go soft, sleep erections have the advantage of occurring during dreams, when a man is completely unaware that his penis is trying to be hard. In one sense, these sleep tests provide information in a pure state, in which the man cannot be nervous about his erections because he has no awareness of them. If no firm erections occur over a two-night period, the test strongly suggests that the problem is physical.

I showed George and Marie the printout of his sleep test, which indicated four erections the first night and five the next. Some of them lasted as long as forty-five minutes. But none was more than 50 percent firm.

"Based on your medical history and the test results, I'm convinced this is a physical problem," I told them. "It's not all in your head."

"What do you mean by *physical?*" he asked. "You think I injured myself on the job or something like that?"

"No, it's probably not from an injury," I answered. "In fact, I doubt there's anything you've done that contributed to this problem. Most likely this is all a result of aging. Not that fifty-eight is old. But as we get older, some things don't work as well, and one of them is the penis. About one out of five men your age can't get a good erection anymore. It's very common, which is part of the reason I'm so busy," I said with a smile.

Surprisingly, George smiled back. It was nice to see. He had been so tight, so guarded until then. He now seemed enormously relieved.

"I didn't think it was all in my head," he said. But it was clear he had been concerned that it *might* have been.

"The good news," I continued, "is that there is a pill that might work really well to help you out. It's called Viagra."

George and Marie looked knowingly at each other. They still gave the impression of being a long distance apart despite sitting close to each other, but I had the sense that they had at least joined the same team.

Marie spoke up. "Doctor, we've talked about this. Of course, we've heard about Viagra. But I'm concerned that it might be dangerous for George. Haven't there been a lot of heart problems when men take Viagra?"

"There were some scary stories when Viagra first came out," I replied. "But they turned out to be completely false. Actually,

Viagra appears to be one of the safest drugs around. Men who take nitrate medications for their heart, like nitroglycerin, should not take Viagra. But George doesn't take any heart medicine, and I think it will be perfectly safe for him to try it. There are a few side effects that some men may experience—for example, a headache, a warm, red face and ears, a stuffy nose, or an upset stomach—but none of these is dangerous. Just a nuisance more than anything else. Also, a few men see a blue haze around lights, but it's a rare side effect and it quickly goes away."

George and Marie seemed cautiously relieved. I gave George a prescription, instructed him on how to take Viagra for the best effect, and asked them to come back to see me in a few weeks.

"Okay, Doc, but is this pill gonna make me . . . well, you know . . . a man again?"

"I can't guarantee it, George, but Viagra does work very often. Some guys say it makes them feel like a new man."

"I guess I'll give it a try. I may as well find out if I've got anything left in the tank," George shrugged, in a way that reminded me of how he had acted when he had first come in. But there was something different about George now. He was ready, even eager, to take some action, in spite of some reservations. That was understandable. After a man fails repeatedly at sex, it takes a lot of courage for him to try yet again and run the risk of humiliation. The anticipation of failure sits like a heavy load on his shoulders.

"Thank you so much, Doctor," Marie said, as they walked out. I wished them well, watched them go, and crossed my fingers that the magic blue pill would fix both George's plumbing and Marie's relationship.

A Serendipitous Discovery

The Viagra story is one of those great tales of serendipity in medicine. When Pfizer researchers first started working with sildenafil, the generic name for Viagra, they hoped it might be useful for patients with heart disease. Acting on a biochemical pathway, sildenafil was a new type of medication known to have significant effects on blood vessels; hence, it might be useful for individuals with clogged heart arteries.

The results were somewhat disappointing. At the end of the early trials, the subjects were asked to return their unused pills, a routine procedure in such studies. Then a strange and wonderful thing occurred: the men who received Viagra rather than a placebo did not want to return their pills. Many of them with blood vessel disease of the heart were impotent because they also had blood vessel disease of the penis. Although the pills did not help their heart disease, their erections, remarkably, were greatly improved. No wonder they did not want to return their pills! Pfizer hit a home run with Viagra in an area of medicine that the researchers had not even considered until the truth behind the reluctant return of medication was discovered.

A Viagra Success

George and Marie returned a few weeks later at their appointed time. George looked ten years younger. I first thought he had dyed his hair or lost some weight, but neither of these proved true. This time he was holding Marie by the hand, not walking in front of her or pushing her back into his shadow. All about him was an aura that conveyed a contentment with life that I suspect he had not had for years. And this time I didn't have to pump him for answers to my questions. As I sat down to join them in the office, he seemed about to burst with excitement.

"Doc, I don't know what's in that pill, but it's amazing." He shook his head, grinning. "The first one I took worked just like you said it would. I feel like a big stud again!" he said, laughing at himself. Marie beamed at me too and then looked back at her new man, her husband of twenty-five years.

As we said our good-byes at the end of the visit, George grasped my hand in his own enormous right hand and held it vice-like for what seemed several minutes. At the same time, he held Marie under the wing of his left arm, pressing her close to his body. It felt like a group hug. George tried to get out the words, "Thank you," but his voice trailed off halfway through. He swallowed the syllable "kew," and his eyes welled up. I watched them walk down the hallway on their way out, George's arm still around Marie, who seemed to have grown in her own way, now filling a space that seemed as large as that of George.

Nice people. Nice result. A feel-good story for them, and certainly for me as well. A story, in truth, that happens every day for many couples, thanks to Viagra. Yet I marvel at what happens with couples such as George and Marie. It is wonderful that a medication can restore George's erections so that he can feel like a real man again, but if we go back to how each partner felt at the beginning of the first visit with me, it is hard to believe that a pill could restore an entire relationship.

And let there be no question that this is exactly what did happen. I received a Christmas card from Marie with a note in which she wrote that George had been warm and affectionate with her to a degree she had not experienced since before their children were born. She and George were planning a long-postponed vacation to the Caribbean in the spring. They planned to relax in the sun, do some sightseeing, and have a couple of weeks of Saturday nights.

The Power of Viagra

A man complains that his plumbing no longer works. A woman complains that her husband will not touch her or show any affection any longer. After treatment, the man's plumbing functions properly for several hours after taking a blue pill, which he takes only a few times a month. The woman then reports that her husband is now affectionate and attentive throughout the week. It continues to astound me that a pill that works on blood vessels can successfully treat a failing relationship. But it's true. This is the power of Viagra. This is the stuff that myths are made of.

Within the simple story line, though, lie powerful lessons about what sexuality means to men and to women and what impact sexuality has on relationships in general. Viagra has become a tool we can use to examine men's and women's sexuality. It provides a window into the psyche of both men and women. The variations that individuals have in their responses to sexual success or failure provide a rich texture to the tapestry of human relationships. The remainder of this book is devoted to examining and learning to appreciate that richness. But first it is important to draw some lessons from the story of George and Marie.

A Woman's Need for Affection

The first thing to notice about George and Marie is that their perspectives on sexuality were vastly different. George saw himself as having a plumbing problem, whereas Marie saw herself as having a relationship problem. On the face of it, both desired the same thing: a return to their old sexual relationship. But this is not what Marie described. She missed something that she saw as affecting the whole fabric of her relationship with George, and not just the physical or sexual touching. Marie craved affection. She also missed being able to think of herself as a successful sexual woman within their marriage, in which she could provide her husband with those special feelings that he experienced only in their marital bed. The loss of George's erection made Marie feel unattractive. This response was compounded by the fact that George never touched her anymore, even outside the bedroom. Moreover, he actively discouraged her attempts to show any physical affection. His response exacerbated her feelings of isolation and abandonment.

George was blind to the entire notion of lost affection and physicality, not to mention Marie's feelings of diminished attractiveness. He was shocked when Marie said so simply that she did not feel pretty anymore. Perhaps it made an impact on him that she was suffering too, and not just in the sense that he had "deprived" her of sex.

A Man's Need to Fulfill Expectations

Of paramount concern to George was that he not build up expectations that he could not meet. The lack of physical touching was an effort on his part to be honorable, to behave, in a sense, according to the dictum, "Be your word."

This was the part that Marie could not understand. Both George and Marie were lost in their own worlds of hurt and despair. They licked their own wounds while not fully understanding what their partner might be experiencing.

Remarkable Viagra

If George and Marie's case history had been presented to a group of couples therapists ten or so years ago, I would have expected them to say that it would take many sessions to treat a case like this one. Furthermore, they would say that it would be difficult to predict whether the outcome would be successful.

After all, the problem is daunting. Each person would need to learn that his or her own view of the "truth" is subjective and that "other truths" exist and are valid, namely those of the partner. The next part of treatment in those days might have been to practice speaking and behaving in accordance with the partner's viewpoint. For example, George would try to be affectionate to Marie despite his failed erection, while Marie would try to put herself in George's position in order to experience that failure through empathy. Finally, the therapists might recommend that George and Marie try nontraditional ways of having sex so that each of them could give and receive pleasure, and in that way perhaps come to a place of mutual understanding and appreciation.

Viagra has turned such an approach upside down. Marie received the affection and attention she craved because George took a pill that worked only on his penis. Her goals were achieved even though George never really worked very hard at seeing the world through Marie's eyes. Solving the physical problem often works because it brings a couple back to the place from where they started. This is successful *only if the starting point is a good place for both partners*. Sometimes a sexual problem creates a situation in which the entire relationship must be reevaluated by both partners. When sex covers up an otherwise troubled relationship, fixing the plumbing is usually not enough to keep a couple together, as we will see later in this book.

Learning from Viagra

Viagra has proved to be a successful means of treating erectile dysfunction in many men, whether the cause is physical or psychological. If the relationship was solid and satisfying to both partners before the problem began, there is an excellent chance that successful treatment of the dysfunction will also result in successful treatment of the relationship. This was the result of treating George's erectile dysfunction with Viagra, which in his case helped restore his relationship with Marie.

Not all couples are so fortunate, however. All too often sexual difficulties reflect more complex issues within a relationship, which are unlikely to resolve simply because a man can take a pill to improve blood flow to the penis.

Lessons

- Men and women experience the world differently and often differ in how they see their own roles within a relationship. These different viewpoints play out in nearly every aspect of a relationship, including sex. Men look for dramatic, action-based solutions—for example, "I'm never going to bother her with sex again!" Women look for solutions that involve the sharing of feelings and validation of their viewpoint—for example, "If only he would recognize that I feel unattractive because he never touches me anymore." Learning to see the world through one's partner's eyes makes it much easier to identify and talk about problems as they arise.

- A sexual dysfunction always has major effects on the rest of the relationship, whether a couple is willing to acknowledge or discuss it. The individuals may successfully adapt, even without discussing the sexual problem, but their relationship will profoundly change as they continue to grow further apart.

- Sex is complicated. When a problem arises, it is often difficult for couples to deal with it on their own. Many individuals are uncomfortable talking about sex at all, and even if they want to, they do not have a language for it that is clear and nonthreatening to the other person in the relationship. Specialists who deal with sexuality can help solve problems that otherwise might threaten the couple's entire relationship.

- Men with erection problems are often caught up in their own drama of failed performance. They fail to see or appreciate the impact of what they do or say (or don't do or say!) on their partners. Women, in contrast, often do not appreciate the impact of a failed erection on their partners; accordingly, they may take the response too personally, thinking, "I'm no longer sexy to him," "It's the weight I've put on," or "He must be sleeping with another woman." When a woman asks repeatedly for reassurance, her partner feels greater pressure and more isolated. He already feels bad, yet he believes he still needs to take care of *her*. The result is, as in George's case, that he may withdraw even further.

- It is very easy for people to experience hurt feelings when the sexual part of their relationship becomes a problem. Marie was certain that George's avoidance of sex with her resulted from what she perceived as the "fact" that she was no longer attractive to him. When he stopped showing her any physical attention at all, his cold shoulder confirmed her fears.

- As a rule, a man feels a responsibility to be a good lover for his partner. When he is unable to function the way he feels he should, his self-image and sense of masculinity suffer immeasurably. A man sees himself as no longer being a good provider.

- Viagra can work for many men whether their erectile dysfunction has a physical or psychological cause, that is, the drug can bring on an erection. But Viagra cannot guarantee that the sexual part of the relationship will improve or that the emotional issues between the man and his partner will be resolved.

Chapter Two

The Viagra Edge

Is Harder Better?

The story of George and Marie in Chapter One shows how Viagra can work very successfully for men whose erectile dysfunction has a physical cause. It can even help solve relationship issues that arise with loving couples like George and Marie, who had a long-term committed and devoted marriage but were suffering problems because of the erectile dysfunction.

But what about men who do not have a true erection problem? Just like the young students at Harvard Medical School who ask me what Viagra can do for them, many men who don't have any actual problems with normal potency have also wondered whether Viagra might turbocharge their penis, transforming them into the sexual superstar of their fantasies.

Here is another element of the Viagra Myth that has pervaded our culture: many young men, nervous or insecure about their sexual prowess and performance, assume that having a guaranteed superhard penis is the ultimate path to happiness. Is this true? Does Viagra actually increase rigidity for men without erection problems? And does an extra-hard penis really reward the man who already functions normally, even if this requires a drug to help him accomplish such a goal? Or is this another Faustian bargain with a profound but hidden cost to pay further down the road?

The Viagra Six-Pack

The ability to have a really firm erection is important to men, especially those who are not yet in a committed relationship and hope to impress a partner with their sexual prowess. Women sometimes laugh at what they see as the simplicity of men. "Why do guys think sex is all about the penis?" they ask. For men, sexual performance corresponds with self-esteem, and with the typical male focus on the penis, greater hardness and rigidity translates into greater performance.

The Viagra Myth plays easily into this mind-set because the word on the street is that Viagra does indeed make a normal erection even firmer. As a physician, I am reluctant to prescribe Viagra to anyone who doesn't truly need it for erectile dysfunction, but I have had many patients and even friends with normal erections who have shared their Viagra stories with me.

A Need for Authenticity

My old high-school classmate Fred, for example, confided that he'd tried Viagra to celebrate his fortieth birthday and couldn't believe what a difference it had made when he and his girlfriend had sex that night. Yet despite having had a wonderful night of lovemaking, Fred announced, "I won't take it again."

"Why not?" I asked.

"It's too hard to live up to!" he said, and we both laughed at his unintentional pun. Then Fred grew serious. "I don't want to be in a situation," he said, "where my girlfriend comes to expect that my penis will be completely firm on command. It would be too much pressure for me. I'm okay the way I am, and I don't want to feel that I need to take a pill in order to make love."

I thought this was an eminently sensible response. Creating an artificial new level of erectile performance is not the best way to sustain an authentic relationship. Fred wanted to be accepted for who he was, without any drug enhancement. But as we shall see, this kind of mature attitude is by no means universal among perfectly healthy men in their quest for sexual prowess.

The Need for Insurance

Not everyone has the same response as Fred. One of my patients, Saul, was forty-eight when he came to see me for a completely different problem: vasectomy reversal. Like many other couples who come to see me for this procedure, Saul was twenty years older than his new wife, Bianca. Saul's sudden need for a vasectomy reversal was typical of older men on their second or even third marriage, who had their tubes tied off after having children earlier in life. Their young new wives usually have no children of their own and would like to start a family.

This was the case with Bianca, who had urged Saul to have the vasectomy reversal. After our conversation about the procedure, I stood up to shake his hand, but he stopped me:

"One more thing, Doctor. I was wondering if you had a six-pack you could give me."

Fred wasn't thirsty for a beer. The six-pack he was asking for was the term used in the Viagra ads for the set of six free pills that physicians were encouraged to give to their interested patients. The "six-pack" was a product ad campaign stroke of genius, evoking two great images of American maleness. The first, of course, is the six-pack of beer. The second refers to the highly desired set of abdominal muscles that stand out as six separate components in only the fittest of men.

"Why do you want Viagra?" I asked him. "Are you having trouble with erections?" I wondered whether Saul had bought into the common false belief that a vasectomy results in diminished sexual ability.

"Not really," he answered without any hesitation. "But I've tried Viagra before, and it works great. Bianca is a lot younger than

You know, I can't say definitely that my penis is actually harder, but it sure seems that way. It makes me feel better."

"How do you know your own erections are okay, then?" I asked.

"Well, I still wake up with good erections. And I can get 'good wood' whenever I masturbate," he said proudly, referring to the slang term for a hard penis.

"How Could I Not Use It?"

"So what's the problem?"

"Something happened that I hadn't planned on. I fell in love. Her name is Sara. I met her at a party, and I was completely taken with her. It's not just that she's beautiful. She's so cool and classy—educated, sophisticated, graceful. She carries herself like a princess, but not in a snobby way. At first, I was thrilled that she seemed at all interested in me. After the third date, we ended up in bed together at her place, and we had great sex. Of course, I'd taken Viagra earlier that night, and everything was fine."

James laughed to himself, almost like a snort, as he thought back.

"Sara and I started seeing each other seriously. Our relationship became very intense very quickly. She got to me. Deep. I'm crazy about this woman. And the sex has been fabulous. I think we must have set some kind of world record. Of course, I used Viagra every time. How could I *not* use it? Sara tells me I'm the great lover she's always wished for, and she's ready to do it with me all the time. She even tells me she loves the way my cock responds to her, as if she could just pull an imaginary string and up it comes. She tells me that it makes her feel good when she sees how much I want her."

"Did you ever think of telling her that you were using Viagra?" I asked.

"Yes, of course. I thought about it all the time. It worried me a lot. I mean, I've told her so many things about myself and my life that I've never told anyone else before. But I just couldn't tell her about the Viagra. I figured she'd be angry with me for keeping it a secret from her. I was afraid she'd be disappointed that I wasn't really the lover I pretended to be."

"Maybe I Don't Need Viagra Anymore"

"You said that your own erections were fine. Did you ever think about stopping the Viagra?" I asked.

"Yes, I did, Doctor," he said. "One time I decided not to take it, just to see what would happen. Once Sara and I became close, I didn't really *like* taking it. I wanted her to like *me*. You know what I mean?" James ran his hands over his slicked-back hair and straightened himself in the chair.

"We had sex that night, and everything was fine. No different really than when I take Viagra. *Maybe* I was just a little bit less hard, but not so much that anyone but me would have noticed. Afterward, I'm thinking to myself, 'Hey, that wasn't too shabby. Maybe I don't need Viagra anymore.' I fell asleep all happy with myself. The idea that Sara might like me just the way I am was so incredible. And I didn't want to be hiding stuff from Sara anymore, especially the Viagra.

"Half an hour later I woke up, and there she was, stroking my penis again. But this time I stayed completely limp. *No way* I was going to get hard. She seemed surprised. If I'd taken Viagra as usual, I would have been ready for her. After a while, she stops trying, gives this little laugh, and says, 'Looks like someone doesn't want to be my big stud anymore.' Then she rolled over and fell asleep.

"She didn't say it in a mean way, but I could tell she was disappointed. Right then I decided I was going back to Viagra. I *wanted* to be her big stud. She'd told me she bragged to her girlfriends about how many times a night we would have sex. I liked the idea that she was proud of me in that way."

Viagra Discovered

"So when did things fall apart?" I asked.

"I was careless," James said. "Sara more or less moved in with me. She still had her own apartment, but she was over at my place all the time. She started doing little things for me around the house. One day I asked her to bring a favorite jacket of mine to the cleaners, and when she cleaned out the pockets, she found a couple of those little blue Viagra pills. It's amazing she didn't find them earlier. I had Viagra pills stashed everywhere, just in case. She asked me what they were.

"I was embarrassed and said 'I'm not really sure what pills you're talking about, but those are probably the allergy pills the doctor gave me last spring.' She bought that explanation for about twelve hours, until she told one of her girlfriends, who laughed at her for being so gullible. Her friend told her that blue diamond-shaped pills help with allergies only if the person is allergic to sex!

"That night Sara asked me point-blank if I'd been taking Viagra, and I had to tell her the truth. She wouldn't talk to me for three days after that. I didn't know what to do with myself. That's why I came home to Boston for a while. I needed to clear my head out."

"Exactly what did Sara say when she found out you were taking Viagra?" I asked

"Why don't you talk to her yourself?" James asked, brightening.

"What do you mean?"

"Sara's here, sitting in your waiting room. She flew out a couple of days ago. She's staying with friends, though. I'd been hoping to have her come to Boston at some point, to meet my parents and friends, but not like this. We've started talking at least, but she's still really upset with me. Would you talk to her?" he asked. "I was hoping you could explain things to her from a man's point of view."

Here was an interesting and unexpected development. It was certainly a good sign for James that Sara had taken the trouble to fly all the way to Boston to spend some time with him, but I could feel the tension building in him as my secretary escorted Sara down the hall to my office.

"I Thought It Was Me That Turned Him On"

Dressed simply in jeans and a lavender button-down shirt, Sara was a very attractive young woman. Like James, she had pulled her long dark hair back into a ponytail.

"I'm not sure why you've asked me to join you two," she said.

"Well, James asked me if it would be all right if you joined our conversation, and I thought it might be helpful for everyone. James was telling me how much he cares for you, but that the two of you have been struggling since you discovered that he'd been using Viagra." I explained.

"Oh. This is all so personal," Sara said, closing her eyes for a moment. "Okay," she said finally. "What would you like to know?"

"Why don't you start by telling me what it was like for you when you learned that James was taking Viagra?" I suggested.

Sara smiled weakly. "I was shocked, to tell the truth. I never suspected it, and it made me feel like a fool for having trusted James so completely. He had acted so sweet to me and always seemed interested in what I had to say. I've never been with a guy before who actually cared so much about what I thought or how I felt." She glanced at James, who looked back at her as if he were a stray puppy searching for a home.

"James was so *into* me, especially with sex. He was always ready to go. I don't mean to sound like I'm pretending to be a virgin or anything, but I never had so much sex before in my life. It felt wonderful to be desired that way.

"When I found out that James was taking Viagra and that he had lied about it, I didn't know what to think. I had been completely naked with him. I don't mean just taking my clothes off. I had let him into the softest places in my heart, and he had been so gentle with me. That's what made me fall in love with him.

"Then I find out he's been lying to me the whole time." Sara shot James a nasty look. I could almost see the steam rising from Sara's head as she vented her anger. "I didn't even know anymore if he found me attractive! All this time I'd thought it was *me* that turned him on. But then I found out it was the Viagra! I was devastated! If he lied about Viagra, maybe he lied to me about everything else. Who knows? What other secrets did he have? Maybe he was pretending to be kind to me when he was really laughing inside."

"Who Is This Man Sitting Next to Me?"

Part of the difficulty was that James and Sara each looked at the problem through different lenses and could not see the other's point of view. James viewed his use of Viagra as a performance issue, whereas Sara saw it as a trust issue. Trust is an essential element to all good relationships, and once lost, it can be difficult to regain.

"So you felt betrayed by James when you learned he was taking Viagra without telling you?" I asked Sara.

"Absolutely! Who *is* James? I have no idea anymore who this man is sitting beside me right now. He would tell me touching stories about learning about life while fishing with his grandfather or being bullied as a small child. He even wrote a song to me. Did he tell you that? It's beautiful." She paused to gather herself. "I thought James had really opened himself up to me. But he didn't even bother to tell me that he had to pop a pill to have sex with me."

She turned in her chair to face James. "What's that all about?" she challenged him. "How do you think it feels to suddenly discover that you need to take a pill in order to get excited with me?" Sara covered her face with her hands, overcome with emotion.

"Sara," James said in a soft voice, reaching out to touch her on the forearm, which she pulled away. "I *am* always excited by you. I've told you that over and over. That's not what the Viagra was about. My desire for you has always been genuine. I took the Viagra because I wanted to make sure I could always give you pleasure. But once you and I started getting serious, I was afraid to stop taking the pills or to tell you about it because I thought you liked the way my penis was always hard."

Sara looked at James again. "Do you have any idea how ridiculous you sound?" she asked, her voice rising. "You think a hard penis makes you a great lover? You just don't get it, do you?"

James looked away, shamed by her words.

Sara softened as she continued. "James, you *are* a wonderful lover. You make me feel close to you. You pay attention to me in all the right ways. You're tender and sweet and fun with me. You don't need any pills to be my honey."

"I Never Believed You Could Actually Love the Real Me"

I brought the conversation back to James's concerns. "James told me that he was afraid that you would be disappointed in him if he stopped using Viagra because his penis wouldn't be as hard and he wouldn't be able to have sex as often."

Sara clutched her head with her hands like a vise. "I cannot *believe* I'm having this conversation! *Of course* I liked it when James was hard. And *of course* I loved it when he was ready to go again almost as soon as we were done. I wondered about that at the beginning, but then I figured I had just shacked up with Superman. It felt great to think that I had finally met someone who was so in tune with everything about me that he was always turned on by me.

"But to tell you the truth, even though all the lovemaking was fabulous at the beginning, after a while, I would go for round two or three mainly because I thought that James needed it. There was one night when we had intercourse only once, and James was grumpy the next morning. I assumed it was because we had done it only the one time. I was kind of relieved, though. I needed the sleep!"

In referring to the night when James did not take Viagra, Sara confirmed how common it is for men and women to share the same experience but come away with a completely incorrect assumption about the other person's reaction. James had been so worried that he had disappointed Sara by not being able to achieve a second erection that he vowed to himself to resume using Viagra. For her part, Sara interpreted James's response as a need on his part to have sex repeatedly every time they were physically intimate.

"Sara, what would you like to see happen now in your relationship with James?"

"I don't really know," she said. She glanced sideways at him. "I just wish he had told me about the Viagra at the very beginning.

I can deal with anything if I feel like someone is being honest with me. But how am I supposed to trust him now?"

"I didn't take the Viagra to fool you, Sara," James interjected. "That night we had sex only once? That was the very night I didn't take Viagra. I was all happy, because the sex was great without it, but when you couldn't get me up again, you said something about my not being your stud anymore. I didn't want to disappoint you again, so I went back to taking Viagra. You don't know how much I'd love to not take it anymore."

James was starting to get worked up himself now. "It's not about keeping secrets from you. I took the Viagra because I thought you liked the way I was with you in bed. I did it for you, not me."

Putting the Best Foot Forward

"You know," I interjected, "I see so many couples pass through my office, but most of them don't have nearly as much feeling for each other as the two of you do. I'm very moved just listening to both of you. And I hope you can find a way to make this work out.

"But let me say something further. Many of us have this fantasy that if we meet the right person, everything will proceed according to this impossibly romantic script: sex will be perfect; we can let go of all our pretenses; we can bare our souls and be accepted unconditionally. It doesn't usually work out that way, though. We start out cautiously, behaving in ways that we think make us more desirable or likable.

"James wanted you to like him, Sara, so he took Viagra in the hope that you would really enjoy sex with him. Then he got stuck. I fully understand why you feel betrayed, and I agree that he should have told you that he was taking the pill. But I can also understand how once you said his lovemaking was so great, he feared that he would disappoint you without the Viagra. Basically James wanted to please you and couldn't figure out how to be honest about it."

"But it feels as if he was pretending the whole time we were in bed together!" Sara complained.

"Well, in my practice, I've come to realize that most of us pretend to some extent at the beginning of a relationship. For some people, this might mean cleaning up the usual mess in our homes in order to appear neat. Or wearing nice clothes instead of sweatpants for the most casual times together. We all do it in a million different ways, and it doesn't mean we're dishonest people. We're just trying to make a good impression."

Sara nodded. "I know what you're getting at. I didn't let James know I smoked until after we'd been together a little while." She paused as she thought about this some more. "But taking Viagra seems a lot different to me than just trying to put your best foot forward."

James cut in. "But that's all I was trying to do . . . except that it wasn't my foot!" Sara laughed, smiling at James for the first time since she'd stepped into the room.

"Well, the question now is whether you two can move forward. Sara, can you see why James became stuck taking the Viagra?"

She nodded.

"Do you think you can try again?" I asked.

"Yes," she said, after a pause. Her eyes locked with James, who looked as if he was ready to cry in relief.

"James, do you understand why Sara was so angry at you?"

He nodded. "She wants me to be straight with her. We know each other a lot better now, and I'm going to try."

"It's not easy, James, but I think you'll find it's worth the effort. The more you open up and let go of trying to do something *in order to* impress Sara, like being a sexual superstud, the more the two of you will be able to enjoy each other."

James and Sara, both with awkward smiles, stood up. James reached for Sara's hand, and she let him take it as they stepped out of the room and walked down the hall toward the exit. As she leaned her head against his shoulder, the leather fringe swaying with each step, I overheard James say, "I think my allergies are all cleared up now."

Learning from Viagra

Is a harder penis better? It may be, depending on the situation. But as in the proverbial deal with the devil, one may have to pay for better performance by giving up one's soul.

James thought that taking a medication to enhance his erection made him more lovable to Sara. Secretly taking Viagra was an acceptable bargain to James because he did not believe he could be loved as he was. He was therefore willing to pretend to be somebody else so that Sara would fall for him.

This shortchanged not only James but Sara too. Ultimately, by believing that Sara could fall in love with him only if he had a hard penis "with an edge," James created a narrow vision of what Sara was all about. He failed to trust Sara's capacity to be an accepting and loving person.

For the man bent only on wooing women without ever choosing to have an emotional relationship, there may be little obvious downside to taking Viagra. He is not putting his lovability on the line in any case. With one-night stands and casual superficial contacts, sex is really little more than a performance, and a man may then be comfortable with the realization that he has taken a performance enhancer. If the only goal is to have good sex, perhaps even acrobatic or thrill-seeking sex, then taking a pill that makes this possible does not create emotional or relationship issues. In these situations, nothing is at stake except the sex act itself.

In James's case, however, it is highly significant that he considered discontinuing Viagra as soon as he felt himself becoming emotionally involved with Sara. He did want her to love his genuine self, but his insecurity stood in the way. Overly focused on his penis as the center of the relationship, James became anxious the night he was unable to achieve a second erection. He imagined his relationship with Sara was now in jeopardy and returned to what he regarded as his magic potion.

No doubt James's firm penis did increase Sara's enjoyment of him. As she said, it's wonderful to feel so attractive and desirable.

Women enjoy sex as much as men do, and a hard penis can contribute to good lovemaking. But Sara fell in love with James because he gave her something precious she hadn't had experienced in relationships before: respect, consideration, and tenderness. She already thought he was a sweetheart. Sara already loved James because of who he was; he just didn't see it.

For some men, relationships are not about emotions, connectedness, acceptance, or lovability. Saul cared only that he could be a vigorous lover for his young wife, Bianca, whom he saw as a trophy, a prize. He was willing to do whatever it took to keep her in his life. For Saul, the issue was his performance, not authenticity. Fred, in contrast, cared more that he could just be himself than to create inflated expectations of what he could do sexually with the aid of a pill.

In romance as in life, it is our imperfections that make us each unique individuals. There is an apt French saying for this: "It is the best feeling in the world to be loved, not in spite of our flaws, but because of them."

Lessons

- Viagra may actually make a normal erection harder for some men. It may also make it easier to achieve a second or even a third erection.

- Having a harder or more responsive erection may be desirable for men who are focused on their sexual performance. It may make them feel more confident and sexier.

- The secret use of Viagra may jeopardize a relationship if it is discovered, by eroding the trust necessary for all good relationships.

- A woman who discovers that her partner is using Viagra may well wonder whether he is taking it because he does not find her attractive enough. However, it is more likely that he is taking Viagra because he is worried about his own sexual performance.

- A man who secretly takes Viagra in order to feel that he is a better lover, and thus more desirable, runs the risk of feeling false and inadequate if he becomes emotionally involved with his partner. He may start to wonder whether he can be loved and appreciated for his own authentic self.

- Women enjoy good sex as much as men do, and a firm erection can contribute to good lovemaking. But a firm penis by itself does not a great lover make.

- When a man uses Viagra secretly because he doesn't trust that his partner will enjoy him as he is, he is assuming that she has a superficial attitude toward love and sex based only on erectile prowess. This narrow view limits the potential for a full and truly loving relationship.

Chapter Three

Performance Anxiety and Viagra

In Chapter Two, we explored the ways in which men strive for an ever-harder erection, even if this means taking a medication like Viagra to help them. This emphasis on sexual performance is a big issue for men. But it is also a double-edged sword, because the dark side of a successful performance is the possibility of failure. When the erection fails because of nervousness, it is called *performance anxiety* or sometimes *psychogenic impotence*.

Unfortunately, many men have experienced at least one episode of performance anxiety at some point in their life. This also means, of course, that a large number of women have been present for the event as well, though their perception of the experience is usually quite different.

The Fear of Failure

The failure to obtain an adequate erection because of performance anxiety can be an excruciating experience, as any honest man will testify. "I felt like a total wimp loser. How could I face her again. It was just devastating," men have told me.

The Viagra Myth is that a little blue pill can solve all erection problems, rendering the disappointment and frustration of performance anxiety a thing of the past. If only it were true. The stories that follow illuminate this aspect of the Viagra Myth and its relationship to performance anxiety.

The Popsicle-Stick Splint

Sitting around drinks one day, a group of friends found the conversation turning to sex. Trudy, a woman in her late thirties, said, "See that waiter over there? Once when I was single, I brought home a guy who looked just like that. He was this gorgeous Italian who spoke with an adorable accent. When he took his clothes off, I thought I had died and gone to heaven. Everything was great until he goes to put on a condom. Then it was 'Pfffft,' like someone had stuck a pin in a balloon, and the whole evening was a loss, no matter what I did. What a waste of manhood!"

Judy spoke up. "I've had that same experience a few times. What is it with guys? They get all excited as if the only thing they care about in the whole world is going to bed with you, and then when you finally get them alone, they can't finish what they started. The first time it happened to me, I couldn't figure it out. Had I done or said something wrong? Had he discovered some repulsive physical flaw of mine that had turned him off so completely?"

Deanna jumped in. "I know exactly what you mean!" The women were all enjoying themselves now, sharing stories of false male bravado and their underlying frailties, while the men at the table listened silently, gamely pretending to be unaffected personally by any of the stories.

"I understand now that it's got little to do with me and all to do with men and their performance issues," she continued. "And I know I'm *supposed* to be understanding. It's just that I don't always *feel* like being understanding. What I *feel* like saying to them is, 'You've been working it all night, and I'm ready for you *now*. If your equipment isn't responding properly, why don't you just get some popsicle sticks and tape them to your penis like a splint so you've got something hard enough to go inside me. You weren't so shy when you got me here all butt-naked!'"

The women were all screaming with laughter at this point, and people were staring at the table to see what the commotion was about. Deanna turned to the men at the table, challenging them as a group. "So tell us, O great warriors of the bedroom, what is a woman to do if her man can't get it up?"

The four men at the table glanced sheepishly around at the others, none particularly interested in volunteering to be the lightning rod for this kind of attention. Finally, Paul spoke up: "I know I speak for all the men here when I say that nothing of this sort would ever happen with any of us!"

"Hear, hear!" yelled the other men laughing, with beer mugs clinking and high-fives all around.

"No, seriously," said Trudy. "What does a woman do in that situation to help the guy out? We never know what to do. We're afraid to be too passive, yet we don't want to put more pressure on you guys by being too aggressive either. If we just roll over and go to sleep, we're afraid you'll feel rejected, and we'll make the situation even worse."

"Needless to say, I have no personal experience with this problem myself," offered Ken, "but I have a 'friend' who told me about something that happened to him a long time ago. Of course, it only happened the one time in his entire life."

"Sure. A *good* friend, right, Ken?" teased Judy.

"He was a teenager when it happened," Ken continued, "and it was the first time he was trying to have sex with this particular girl. They were at her home, and her parents were out for the evening. Just as he was about to go inside her, he heard a noise and thought her parents were coming home. It was a false alarm, but by now it was too soft to go in. It was like trying to play pool with a limp noodle."

"What did the girl do?" asked Trudy.

"She tried everything, but to tell you the truth, once the penis went soft, it didn't matter what she did. It was as if she wasn't even in the picture anymore, except as the target where he needed to hit a bull's-eye."

"I know that feeling where the guy just disappears into his own brain," said Judy. "Once this guy is walking around my bedroom with his head hanging after things weren't, um, progressing, and he's just talking to himself as if I weren't even in the room. I got fed up, waved at him, and said 'Yoo-hoo! Remember me?'"

"It wasn't about you anymore, Judy. It was all about the guy's penis at that point," explained Laurence, as if he had some personal insight into the experience.

"Exactly!" said Deanna. "One more example of the misguided male thought process. They just think too much when it comes to their penis. I learned to just jump on a guy when I first start in with him so that he doesn't have time to think about it and get nervous. Thank goodness Viagra is around now to help the weaker sex."

"Amen to that!" exclaimed Mark, who had been strangely quiet up to this point, and everyone laughed.

The Male Performance Imperative

Ours is a society focused on performance. We look up to those who have what Ernest Hemingway, himself the heavyweight champion of supermacho authors, called grace under pressure, like Mayor Giuliani of New York City after the terrorist attacks on the World Trade Center, or President Kennedy staring down the Russians during the Cuban missile crisis. We even treat our best athletes as heroes, particularly those who are "clutch performers"—those men and women who come through at times of greatest pressure: the one who takes the last shot as the game is on the line and the scoreboard ticks off the last seconds.

At the other end of the spectrum are those individuals who perform poorly under the hot lights of observation. These poor men and women, sometimes no older than boys or girls, are said to "choke." Bill Buckner was an otherwise decent Boston Red Sox player who botched an easy play during the World Series in 1986, and the Red Sox went on to lose a championship that had appeared all sewn up for them. Although Bill Buckner must have excelled throughout his life in order to make it to such a high level in baseball, he was reviled afterward in Boston and is remembered now only as the player who choked, "a loser."

It is a narrow view of life when one sees only two possibilities with any opportunity: to be the hero or to be the goat. Yet this is often how men see themselves. "If I succeed, I'm a winner: if I fail,

I'm a loser." Boys grow up with fantasies of being in do-or-die situations. This is what propels fantasies of heroic wartime rescues, critical athletic moments where there is one last chance for success, and even comic book scenarios. When I was a child, I used to imagine that I was Superman trying to avert global disaster as a huge meteor hurtled toward earth. This boyhood "training" can create pressure-cooker situations out of ordinary circumstances. A woman may not understand why her husband becomes so agitated and sweaty as he fights traffic trying to get to the airport on time. But she never incorporated into her essence the unspoken rule governing a variety of male actions: success is critical because "the fate of the universe hangs in the balance." A woman may be upset if the couple arrives late to the airport because of the practical problems that stem from this, but she may be stunned by the man's reaction, as if he has failed in his manly duty and is thus a "loser."

One of the few human endeavors that fails to improve with concentration and determination is creating an erection. "Relax, relax" is easy to say, but completely counterintuitive for a man when things are going wrong sexually. Moreover, the moment a man has any doubt that he is performing well sexually, he is likely to panic at the inevitable thought that his penis might not work at all on this occasion and that he will be unable to complete what he sees as an all-important event.

A Woman's Power to Heal

When a man and woman have gone through the buildup leading to a sexual encounter and the penis fails to respond or, even worse, the erection disappears just before "the moment of truth," it is disappointing to the woman as well. While the man tries to figure out how to deal with this embarrassing situation, the woman must deal with her own set of issues. Not only may she feel frustrated, but she may even feel as if she needs to play the part of an amateur psychologist in order to salvage the situation, by helping the man achieve an erection again or feel okay so that they can try again another time. As Laurence said, this may not be easy for the woman to do once the erection has failed, because the man may be so focused on his own drama.

But some women tell remarkable stories about how a failed erection moved their relationships forward. "I knew Sean as a friend for quite some time before we started dating, and I really cared for him," began Bonnie, "but the first time we went to bed together, I could tell he was nervous, and it just didn't work out. I was disappointed, naturally, but I felt worse for Sean. He always acted like this cool, tough guy, but he seemed so sad the way he was sitting on the edge of the bed.

"Finally, I took his arm and pulled him toward me, saying 'I'm so cold. Please come close and keep me warm.' When he lay back down, I snuggled into him and told him all the things I liked about him. When I told him I thought he was really sweet, he looked up at me and said, 'Really?' like he couldn't believe it. Then I told him I didn't need to have sex with him that night, but I did want to be able to lie close to him and to feel his hands and body on me.

"We had a wonderful night. Sean was tender with me in a way I had never imagined he could be. He had always been kind of macho when we had kissed before, as if he was playing a role right out of some gangster movie, but not that night. He was like a sweet puppy dog, kissing me all over. It didn't take long before he had a great erection, but I was enjoying Sean so much that I wouldn't let him put it in for the longest time. When I finally let him, it was fantastic for both of us. Sean still acts tough in public and around his buddies but never with me. We got engaged a couple of months later.

"I think Sean just needed to hear that I liked him for who he really was, and then the penis took care of itself."

As Bonnie's story so nicely demonstrates, if the goal of sex is intimacy rather than performance, then the absence of a firm erection need not interfere with lovemaking. Indeed, in some cases, it may provide an opportunity for different types of pleasurable interactions, both physical and emotional.

"It's All in My Head"

When men hear the term *psychogenic impotence*, they often translate it into casual language: "Oh I get it. You think it's all in my head." Although this is true, because the problem *is* all in their head, it doesn't mean they are *crazy*. People have this idea that a man with a psychological cause for his impotence must have had a strange relationship with his mother when he was four years old, or that he needs to be dressed up in women's clothing in order to achieve an erection. Those cases do exist, but they are quite rare. All it really means is that the anxious thoughts are getting in the way of the body's usual response to a sexual situation. Instead of the blood vessels within the penis filling up with blood, the adrenaline release that accompanies anxiety makes the blood vessels constrict, like a kinked hose, and the penis then fails to become firm.

It amazes me how evolution has created the wonderful biological system that we call the human body. One of the strongest responses in the body is the reaction to fear, called the fight-or-flight response. My colleague, Dr. Alan Altman, has a nice way of explaining how the fight-or-flight response applies to male sexuality. Imagine if, as a caveman, you were confronted suddenly with a saber-tooth tiger. Your choices are two: to battle it out ("fight") or to run away ("flight"). Adrenaline is released throughout the body to help in this situation by increasing the heart rate and blood pressure, which helps to pump oxygen to the brain and the large muscles of the arms, legs, and torso.

But having a stiff penis would only get in the way with either running or fighting. Part of the fight-or-flight response is thus to make sure that the penis stays soft. Since anxiety is a trigger for the fight-or-flight response, this explains why being nervous in a sexual situation leads to poor or absent erections.

The medical world is still a little confused about psychogenic impotence. Although Viagra has been shown to be particularly effective for men with a "shy penis," many physicians still believe that men should work through this problem on their own rather than take medication for it.

I recently lectured to a group of 120 Danish physicians who were visiting the United States and described two cases to them. One was a married man in his sixties who had progressive difficulty with erections over several years and had high blood pressure as well as diabetes, both of which can contribute to erectile dysfunction on a physical basis. The second case was a young, healthy single man who was unable to achieve an erection with a new partner because of anxiety and who then continued to have difficulty for several weeks. When I asked how many of the audience would offer to treat the first man with Viagra, every hand went up. When I asked about the second man, only three hands were raised.

This response surprised me somewhat, since the young man has a better chance of a successful result with Viagra than the older man did. But this episode reinforced my impression that the medical community is still resistant to the idea that healthy men should take any form of medication to help with sex. Their attitudes instead are that the man should somehow work it out on his own, as if he just hasn't tried hard enough. Or maybe it just wasn't meant to be. But in any case, nearly all of these doctors thought that they shouldn't be getting involved in such cases.

I disagree entirely with this attitude. Men with psychogenic impotence suffer greatly from their inability to have satisfying sexual relationships. It is wonderful that we live in an age where there is a safe and effective medication that may help. Nevertheless, as we shall see, sometimes Viagra works, and sometimes it doesn't.

When Does It Work, and When Does It Not?

Here are two examples of recent cases where I've tried to use Viagra for men with performance anxiety.

The Big Buildup

Matt was forty-one and had been dating Melissa, age thirty-four, once or twice a week for almost two months.

Matt told me this story plainly, always maintaining eye contact with me. "Melissa was so sexy, and she would get me so excited. But she had a thing about going 'all the way.' She wanted to be sure, she said, before she gave herself to me. That's how she put it—'gave herself to me.' I was feeling like it was all a little silly and even thought about ending our relationship, but Melissa finally said, 'Okay, in three Saturdays, we'll do it.'" She kept talking about it and e-mailing me about it: 'Be ready for me!' she would say.

"When the day finally came, I *was* ready. Or so I thought. Melissa was to come meet me at my apartment at 10:00 A.M. I was waiting for her in my best pajamas. I figured we were going to go straight to bed and get busy. But she was dressed in nice clothes and had put on makeup, like we were going out to dinner at a fine restaurant. I tried to take her into the bedroom—I'd been waiting and waiting, after all, just for this moment—but she wasn't ready yet.

"'Can I have a drink first?' she asked me.

"'But it's only ten o'clock in the morning!' I exclaimed.

"'Please,' she asked again. 'Do you have any red wine?'

"After a drink and some frustrating small talk, I tried getting her into the bedroom again, but she wouldn't go. She made some comment about my not having gotten dressed yet. So even though it was only about 11:00 A.M. on a Saturday, I went into my room, changed into a suit and tie, and came back out to the living room. She smiled, told me I looked nice, and asked for another glass of wine. After another twenty minutes or so, she took my hand and led me to the bedroom. I figured, 'What the heck, women are weird, but I'm finally learning how to play the game right.' Was I ever wrong on that last score!

"We step into the bedroom, and Melissa starts to take off my tie and undo my shirt. I'm starting to get excited now. She won't kiss me yet, though, which was odd, because that was the one thing she'd always been happy to do with me. I start to try to take off her shirt, and she stops me, saying, 'Not yet. It's too bright in here.'

"It's true; it *was* bright. It was daytime, after all, and a sunny day too. My blinds didn't block the sun too well, but that had never bothered me. But it sure bothered Melissa. So picture this: we both end up balancing on the radiators, taping blankets over the windows in my bedroom to cut out the daylight! I'm standing there in my underwear, and she's still wearing her nice clothes.

"Finally it was dark. So then she wanted a candle. I go into the kitchen to get a utility candle and light it. Now she's happy. She pulls off her clothing, and she is absolutely ravishing. I'd never seen her naked before. She pulls me onto the bed. I'd been waiting for this moment for so long. But I couldn't get it up. Nothing. Zilch. Nada. After all that buildup too."

"So, what happened?" I asked.

"Well, she worked on me for a long while. I felt stupid. I felt like my body had betrayed me. I'd been an athlete in school and could always rely on my body. But that day, it let me down. I felt like I didn't really want to be there. I would have preferred to go for a run and work up a sweat. Finally, she says, 'I think you need a bath to relax you.'

"She gets me into the bath. Brings in the candle. Starts soaping me with a washcloth. It felt good. She gets in the tub behind me and washes my back. Before you know it, I get a little hard. Melissa climbs around, straddles me, and gets me inside. We had sex that way, even though I was never completely firm.

"It wasn't a complete failure, you know, but it was embarrassing. I liked thinking of myself as a sexually successful guy, but I was pathetic that day. She said, 'Don't worry about it,' but I felt lousy.

"We've tried to do it a few times since then, but it's never been good. Sometimes I'm hard enough to go inside, but I'm thinking the whole time about whether I'm going to lose it completely. Most of the time, it won't get up at all. Even weirder is that I can ejaculate sometimes, even though my penis isn't hard. Is that normal?"

"It can happen," I answered. "Ejaculation has a separate set of controls from erection and can take place even when the blood vessels in the penis don't fill up all the way."

"I know I'm not impotent, Doctor. I got freaked out when this happened and worried that something had happened to my body. I know it doesn't sound too nice, but I was going crazy, and so I called up an old girlfriend and visited with her a couple of times.

Everything worked out great. I don't like her as much as I do Melissa, but she and I had always been in tune with each other sexually. She never made me put up with that first-time crap. Anyway, that's how I know this is all mental for me."

"Well, it seems you've made an accurate diagnosis for yourself. How can I help you?" I asked.

"Doctor, I'm really sweet on Melissa, despite our problems. And maybe I just want to know that I can get it right sexually with her. I don't know. But I was wondering if you thought Viagra might help me out with her."

I went over the rest of his medical history and gave him an examination. Everything was in order. I prescribed Viagra.

Matt came back to see me the following month. He smiled when I walked into the room.

"How are you, Matt?" I asked.

"Great, Doctor. Thank you for the Viagra. It worked! The ship has been righted! I used it only a few times, and then I figured I didn't need it anymore. I'm back to normal. Now that the sex is okay, though, I have to figure out whether Melissa is right for me in other ways. I just received a job offer in Seattle, to start in another two months, and Melissa and I are trying to decide whether she should come out to be with me."

Matt was the best kind of Viagra cure. Once he regained his confidence in his own ability to have sex, he didn't need the medication at all anymore. Unfortunately, it doesn't always work out that way.

A Viagra Failure

William was a thirty-year-old muscular man whom I'd originally met when he did some contracting work on my house. One day, long after the job was completed, he called me at the office and told me he was having sexual problems with a new girlfriend. His regular doctor had prescribed Viagra, but it hadn't helped.

I was surprised, since sudden difficulty with erections in a healthy man is almost always a psychological problem, and as we saw with Matt, Viagra is usually effective in that situation. I wondered if William was taking the Viagra properly.

"William," I said over the phone, "I'm about to leave town and won't be able to see you in the office for at least a week. In the meantime, let's see if we can't get things working for you right away. This sounds situational, related to something going on between you and your new friend Julie. Viagra usually works for this, so let's make sure you're taking it properly. What dose are you taking?"

"I started with one pill, 50 milligrams, and then when it didn't work, I took two of them, 100 milligrams, the next time."

"How many times have you taken 100 milligrams?"

"About four or five times now."

"Do you give the medicine time to get into your system?"

"Yeah. I do what my regular doctor told me to do: I take it at least one hour before we try to have sex."

"Good. Do you take it before or after meals?"

"I haven't paid any attention to food," said William. "Is that important?"

"Yes, it is. If you take Viagra with anything in your stomach, even alcohol, it can slow down how quickly the medicine is absorbed. It may not work as well, or it may just take a lot longer before it starts to work. Some guys who take it after a heavy dinner don't notice any effect until the next morning."

"I didn't know that," he said.

"Tell you what," I said. "Why don't you try the Viagra a few times again, 100 milligrams, and call me next week. If things aren't right, we'll make arrangements to see you in the office. Pay attention to the food issue. My suggestion is that if you guys are going out for the evening, you take the Viagra about thirty to sixty minutes before you start eating and drinking. It stays in your system for a good six hours, so if you took the pill at 6:00 P.M., for example, you're probably all set until midnight or so.

"I really think that you're just freaked out by the whole thing right now, and that if you have one or two successes with Viagra, you won't need it anymore."

I hadn't had time to get into too much detail on the phone with William, but he did tell me that he and Julie had been successful sexually twice, then not at all. There was no question in my mind that there was nothing wrong with William on a physical basis and that the problem stemmed from something that had happened between William and Julie. William was young and healthy, and had normal erections right up until the moment of his difficulties. When a man starts having troubles suddenly, there are only a few possibilities as to what may be causing it: new medications or increased dose of a medication, new major medical events such as surgery, or a bad accident—or the problem is situational.

By situational, I mean there's something about the man's situation that isn't right. It may be anxiety or feeling awkward. Perhaps he is angry at his partner. Perhaps the woman is angry at the man and thus not providing the usual sexual signals that give the man the encouragement he needs.

In any case, I was confident that Viagra would work for William. A study presented at the national urology meeting showed that 40 percent of men who said that Viagra didn't work for them could have success if they were instructed properly in its use. The biggest issue is to take it on an empty stomach. Because William hadn't paid attention to this, I thought there was an excellent chance of success if he took the dose before meals.

William called me again the next week. "It's no better," he said. "I did exactly what you told me, but I don't notice anything different with the Viagra. It's like trying to stuff a marshmallow through a keyhole."

"Let's see if there's anything physically wrong," I told William over the phone. I arranged for him to undergo some tests and then to see me afterward.

William came to my office the next week. We shook hands again. "Thanks for seeing me," he said. "It's strange to see you as my doctor, but it's cool. This is hard stuff to be talking about, but at least I know that I can trust you."

"I know it's a little strange, but it's okay," I said, smiling. "This is what I do," and I invited him to sit down. "William, you've told me a little on the phone, but why don't we start by having you tell me what's been going on with you and Julie."

"There's not much to tell," he said. "I met Julie about two months ago, and we hit it off right away. Sex was fine the first two times we did it, but the third time we got together, my penis never came up at all. I can't explain it. I wasn't nervous or anything. It just didn't happen. We've tried a million times since then, with and without Viagra, and I'm never really hard with her. Every once in a while, I get semihard, enough to get in, but it's a disaster. It just doesn't want to get hard."

"Was there something different that third time with Julie?" I asked.

"Not that I can think of."

"Are you taking any medications at all?"

"None."

"Have you had any injuries around the penis or between your legs, like falling on the crossbar of a bicycle, or something like that?"

"No."

"Have you woken up with an erection in the morning or in the middle of the night since you've started seeing Julie?"

"No, Doctor, and that's part of what's making me crazy. I'm afraid there's something wrong with me. Everything is just different!"

"Can you masturbate and get a firm erection that way? Recently, I mean."

"I've tried, Doctor, I've tried. It kind of works that way. Not great, but it's there. I've done it with and without Viagra. But it's almost as if the penis doesn't have the same feeling anymore, like it's dead. I'm afraid there's something wrong down there."

I gave William a physical examination. He was in great shape, very muscular, and with an all-over tan he achieved by going to the tanning salon on a regular basis.

"William, there's something I'm not getting here. Your physical examination is normal. I've looked over your test results too, and everything is in order. In fact," I said, showing him a graph, "this is the nighttime test you took with the bands on your penis that record any erections. Each night, the body tries to achieve several erections, associated with dreams. You can't be nervous when you're asleep, so we get, in a sense, a picture of your 'pure' erection. If you look here, you can see that you had four erections each night, with some of them lasting as long as forty-five minutes. Most important, you had excellent rigidity during those erections."

"I don't get it. What does this mean?" he asked.

"It means that when your brain isn't thinking about how you're doing, your penis is able to achieve excellent erections. The blood vessels and nerves in your penis are just fine, but not even Viagra can give you an erection if your mind says no."

"So there's nothing wrong with me physically, is that what you're saying?"

"Right."

William sat back in his chair, reflecting on this information. "I *guess* that's a good thing." He was quiet for a moment. "So this is all in my head? Is that what you're saying?" he said more calmly.

"Yes. Tell me again what happened that third time with Julie. I think that's where the secret lies. I'm certain there was something different that third time. What do you remember about that night?"

William looked down at his open hands, sighed, and looked up at me. "Can I be honest with you?" he asked. He gulped. "Truth is, I kinda feel like I'm out of my league with Julie. She's aggressive sexually in a way that I'm not used to. One night when we had first started seeing each other, I was driving her home and she starts unbuttoning my shirt while I'm driving on the highway, rubbing her hands all over my chest while nibbling at my neck. It was amazing we didn't drive into a tree.

"That third night that things didn't work out? We were having drinks, and she asked whether I'd ever been with more than one woman at a time. I've *never* done anything wild like that. In fact, I don't think I'm very wild at all. I asked her back if she'd been with more than one guy, and she tells me about this party she'd been to a few years back. She'd been drunk and took a nap in one of the bedrooms. Two guys came in to talk to her, and she ended up doing it with both of them at the same time.

"I think she thought it would get me excited, but it bothered me. I don't think I'm a prude, but I didn't want to hear about her with other guys, especially doing stuff like that. I could never do that. I'd be too nervous. Listening to her made me feel like I was an uptight stiff."

William paused. He flexed his chest muscles and arms, stretched, and looked up at me with a sheepish smile. "This is probably the kind of thing you were getting at, isn't it?" he asked.

"Have you ever considered the possibility that Julie might be spending time with you because she likes you?" I asked.

William laughed loudly. "That's too obvious! No, I never even considered that. I have this crazy idea that a woman would be interested in me only if I have something special to offer, like my Harley motorcycle or big biceps from working out at the gym. She still tells me stories about sex with other guys and asks me about my experiences. I've always loved sex, and it's always felt exciting to me at the time, but my stories all seem dull compared to hers. And I feel weird telling them in the first place. I don't think it's right for us to talk about sex with old lovers. Maybe I *am* uptight. Julie acts as if it's important to be open about this stuff, but it gives me the willies. What do I do about it?"

"Have you ever told her that?" William shook his head no. "Tell her to stop. Tell her it makes you crazy to think about her having sex with other men. She should be flattered. But the important thing is that you need to do what it takes so that you can be comfortable with her." I let this sink in before I continued. "Let me get something straight, William. Apart from the sexual stuff, do you like Julie?"

"Yes."

"Why?"

"We have a great time together, Doctor. We're always laughing. We like to do a lot of the same things."

"Good. Does she know you're here with me today?"

"No way."

"Does she know you've tried Viagra?"

"No."

"Okay. Here are my recommendations. First of all, tell her you came to see me. Let her know this has been important enough for you so that you decided to see a specialist. It will free you from the pressure of keeping a secret. Give her a chance to be your ally instead of your obstacle. Next, it is critical that you have sex only when you are feeling like having sex."

"I don't get what you mean. I *always* feel like having sex."

"I don't believe that. In fact, I bet you almost never really, truly feel like having sex with Julie anymore. Most guys in your situation have lost that loving feeling. But I am also sure that there are some times that you *do* feel at least a little aroused by her. Those are the times you should try.

"It's a funny thing about Viagra," I continued. "A lot of guys think that Viagra will give them the erection they want, no matter the circumstances. But it's not true. A man needs to be sexually excited if Viagra is going to work. Viagra does not work for men who feel that sex is a chore!"

The next morning, my secretary came to my office to tell me that William was waiting to see me. William was smiling from ear to ear. "I'm sorry to bother you, especially without an appointment," he blurted out, "but I had to tell you what happened. After I left your office, I went to find Julie. I told her I didn't want to hear anything anymore about any other guys. I told her it freaked me out to hear about that stuff. I even told her that it made me feel inadequate, like I wasn't wild enough for her tastes."

William paused to catch his breath. "It was amazing what happened afterward. She started crying and telling me over and over that she was sorry. She said she was just trying to impress me, because she figured I'd been with a lot of women. She said she liked the fact that I hadn't been so wild, that maybe she could trust me, unlike previous men in her life. She said she just liked spending time with me. She snuggled up next to me so tight while she was talking and crying, and I got this terrific hard-on. We ended up having an incredible day and night of sex. And guess what?" William raised both arms straight to the ceiling as if signaling a touchdown. "No Viagra," he shouted.

"William, you're cured!"

Learning from Viagra

The male preoccupation with sexual performance can create enormous anxiety, which may make it impossible for the penis to function at all. When this happens, men tend to see their failure in dramatic terms and may feel that their inability to achieve an erection at one given time means that they are a loser or inadequate. The next time a man tries to have sex, he is likely to be worrying if the penis will respond properly, which may make the situation even worse.

Viagra can be an effective treatment for many men with this type of erection problem. If there is sexual excitement present, Viagra will help the penis achieve good rigidity. Matt was a great Viagra cure because he needed to take it only a few times before he regained confidence in himself sexually. Many men say that just feeling their penis becoming hard makes them more excited, and Viagra may help in this way too.

Some single men who are on the dating circuit use Viagra every time they start a new sexual relationship in order to avoid the frustration and embarrassment that they may have experienced in the past with a "shy penis." Although this is not a standard medical indication for the use of Viagra, I have no objections to prescribing it for this situation. It makes perfect sense to me. But I also recommend that if these men want to continue the relationship, a time comes when they should tell their partners that they're taking Viagra and why, so they can talk through some of the issues or anxieties and see if continuing this medication is really necessary in the long run.

The Viagra Myth is that a pill can solve all our sexual problems. But life is more complicated than this. William had lost his sexual feeling when he was with Julie, and Viagra couldn't help him because the feeling just wasn't there. Instead of feeling aroused, he felt as if he needed to get over a hurdle. Sex was a challenge, and he approached it the way he would a weight machine at the gym: with hard work. Once William was honest and open with Julie and she responded favorably, the sexual feeling came back, and he didn't even need Viagra.

Curiously, some women have found that the man's inability to achieve a firm erection provides an opportunity for a different type of connecting: one in which the man is more vulnerable and in some ways more accessible to them emotionally. Being accepting of the man, whether or not he is "performing well," can unleash in him a flood of warm, positive feelings, which is likely to cause warmth and firmness in the penis as well.

Lessons

- Men too frequently see sex as a performance rather than as a shared activity with their partner. Unfortunately, this creates pressure for a man, which may make it difficult for him to achieve an erection. This is called performance anxiety or psychogenic impotence.

- A number of things can contribute to an occasional failed erection, including stress, alcohol, recreational drugs, fatigue, and relationship problems.

- If a man has failed at achieving an erection one time, it is inevitable that the next time he tries, a part of his brain will be busy assessing whether the penis is hard enough and wondering if it will work properly. Naturally, this process interferes with sex and makes it even more difficult to achieve a good erection. If a man fails a few times in a row, he is likely to lose all confidence in his ability to perform sexually.

- Men tend to think too much about their penis. Many women have learned that if their male partner is in the dumps about his psychogenic erectile dysfunction, they will do well to jump straight to penetration before he has time to think himself out of his erection!

- Viagra can be an effective "jump-start" for many men who have psychogenic erectile dysfunction.

- Viagra does not solve the underlying issues in relationships that may precipitate the difficulty in lovemaking. The best solution is often to clear the air by discussing what feels bad to each person.

- A failed erection may turn out to be an opportunity for a different kind of physical and emotional intimacy that may truly benefit a relationship.

Chapter Four

Viagra and Desire

"Doctor," began Geoffrey, a dapper sixty-seven-year-old English-man, "I wonder if you would be so kind as to give me a prescription for Viagra? I seem to have misplaced my sexual desire. I don't feel quite the same without it, and I was hoping you could help me find it again." There was nothing otherwise wrong with Geoffrey: he just wanted to feel like his younger, previously lustful self.

Here is another aspect of the Viagra Myth: the idea that taking a pill can change who we are in the realm of sexual desire. And make no mistake about it. The feeling of being "highly sexed" and always ready for some "action" is important to the masculine self-image of many men. Even a man who knows he would never have the courage to approach a woman values the idea of having the hunger and capability to be a sexual beast, if only circumstances were a little different. The decline in desire generates concern in men that something is wrong in their world.

In the past, men would do what they could to restore their sexual selves: throw themselves into strenuous physical exercise routines, change their diets, start a vitamin supplement regimen, or all of the above. Today, there is a pill that has garnered worldwide attention as the sexual savior of mankind: Viagra.

How well does Viagra actually work for men who have experienced a decline in their sexual desire? The answer depends to a great extent on the cause of the diminished desire. If desire has been stifled or deflated because of performance anxiety or the embarrassment of authentic erectile dysfunction, then Viagra may be very helpful. Viagra restores desire in this situation by allowing the man to again experience sexual success. However, Viagra will not help desire if there is a deficiency of testosterone or if the problem is the result of side effects of medications. Moreover, if the lack of desire is due to an underlying problem in the individual or the relationship, Viagra cannot provide the mythical cure.

"Surely everyone understands that," said a dinner companion, scoffing at the notion that men would believe Viagra would be a solution for interpersonal issues. But my experience is that many men do *not* understand it. Men regularly ask me for Viagra to help with their lack of desire, while having remarkably little insight into what is going wrong with themselves or in their relationships. Part of the reason is that men have a tendency to be detached from their feelings, unaware that they may even be depressed about something, or seething at their partner beneath their calm manner.

But part of the problem is that as a culture, we are still enamored with the easy fix, the idea that a magic pill will solve our troubles. In the sexual domain, this translates to a demand for Viagra. Certainly, it is easier to take a pill than to do the messy job of working on deeper identity and relationship issues.

The Desire Dilemma

There is a wonderful scene in the movie *Annie Hall* in which the character played by Woody Allen complains to his psychotherapist that he and his girlfriend almost never have sex. At the same moment, the girlfriend, played by Diane Keaton, is complaining to her own therapist that they are constantly having sex. Both psychiatrists ask how often they actually engage in sex, and both characters give the same answer: three times a week. They agreed on the fact but had entirely different experiences as to whether this was too little or too much sex.

This standard male-female lore asserts that the man is always hungry for sex and the woman is put upon by the man's constant sexual craving. Although this stereotype has at least a grain of truth in it for many couples, especially in the younger years, it is by no means universal. As women have freed themselves of the puritanism that suggested that women should not be interested in sex, and "good girls don't," they have become increasingly able to come to terms with their own sexuality and to feel free to express their sexual desire. As a result, it is no longer uncommon for the woman to be the one who initiates sex or to desire it more frequently than her male partner.

Once men emerge from the hormone-induced, sex-addled period of the teenage years and early twenties, sexual desire may still be strong but is no longer so compulsive. Life comes into play, and as men take on responsibilities of work, wife, and parenthood, they often discover that sexual desire may lose the imperative that it once held. I once had a patient who had been married for fifteen years who was unable to have sex during the week, but had no difficulty when he and his wife escaped on the weekends to their country home.

"In the city, I always feel pressured, and I can't get my brain to stop thinking about work and my to-do list. It's only in the country that I can relax and allow sexual thoughts to enter my mind," he explained.

Many couples find reassurance that their sex lives are all right by the resurgence in sexual activity that so often accompanies vacations. Whether it is due to the change in scenery, the distance from stress and problems, or just having an opportunity to become reacquainted with each other, desire frequently becomes strong again for couples during time away from home. Some women have learned that a change of one type or another is the key to stoking new fires in their partners, for instance, by wearing a new piece of lingerie to bed, going away together on a brief vacation, or carving out time alone in their hectic schedules.

There is no set frequency for how often a man or woman should desire sex because of the wide variation in what constitutes normal sexuality. As a physician, I start to be concerned when I hear that there has been a change in a man's own level of libido or if his partner has noticed a change. If this has happened, then it is time to ask why and try to determine if the problem is related to relationship issues, life stresses, depression, hormonal changes, or medications.

A decline in desire may also be an indicator to a man that he is getting old. Guys don't like this idea, especially the baby boomers, who feel that there is no reason on God's green earth that they should lose one iota of the physical blessings they've enjoyed for the first fifty years of their lives. If you don't believe me, check out the ages of some of the guys doing mountain biking, triathlons, and even more extreme sports these days.

In the cultural spirit of "better living through pharmacology," many men who are starting to feel the decline have latched onto Viagra to help them maintain their sexual vigor and their level of sexual frequency and desire. Here, then, is another aspect of the Viagra Myth: that a pill can restore an older man's level of sexual desire to that of a twenty year old. How does reality stack up against this mythology?

The Myth Versus Reality

A forty-seven-year-old financier involved in leveraged buyouts described his thoughts regarding Viagra and desire. "I have great respect for Viagra," he said. "I saw an interview with Hugh Hefner, who must be pushing eighty years old, and he had these two beautiful blonde twins on each arm. The interviewer asked him how he manages to keep going sexually after all these years, and Hefner answers: 'Viagra.' The interviewer then asked what explained his strong sexual appetite at an age when most men have given up on sex altogether, and Hefner just says 'Viagra.' I've never taken it, but if Viagra gives Hugh Hefner that kind of desire, then it gives me hope that I can be a hungry wolf forever too."

We associate a high level of sexual desire with power. As a culture, we almost expect to hear stories about the wealthy and their sexual escapades. We even extend this to our presidents, the Clinton-Lewinsky scandal notwithstanding. As stories emerged after President Kennedy's death, his sexual trysts, for example, with Marilyn Monroe, only added to his mystique rather than diminishing it. Action heroes in the movies appear willing and able to have sex many times a day, no matter how close they seem to be at death's door. James Bond is as good an example of this as any.

Medical Basis

On a medical basis, Viagra has nothing to do with sexual desire. Viagra can help with blood flow to the penis, but it is not an aphrodisiac, and there is no evidence that it has any effect on the part of the brain that controls sexual desire and behavior. Viagra does not on its own create sexual desire or a burst of passion or libido where there has been none before. That's not what it does and not what it's for.

One of the more common causes of reduced sexual desire is the widespread use of the antidepressants called serotonin reuptake inhibitors, such as Prozac, Zoloft, and Paxil. Although these medications are highly effective, they do have the common side effect, for both men and women, of reducing sexual desire. There is yet another sexual side effect that affects both men and women that can be quite troubling: it can make it difficult to achieve an orgasm.

Viagra does not do anything to counter these effects, and using Viagra to treat lack of desire in an individual taking one of those medications is a waste of time. A much better course of action for someone experiencing a sexual side effect from these or any other medications is to speak to one's doctor about it, since in many cases it may be possible to change medications and avoid the sexual problems.

Nevertheless, there *can* be some circumstances where Viagra *does* work to restore sexual desire in men, as demonstrated by Ted in the following story.

"I'm Here to Make My Wife Happy"

Ted was sixty-two years old when he came to see me. One of the questions on the standard medical questionnaire that I ask all patients to complete before their first visit with me asks, "What is the main reason for your visit to the doctor?" Ted had written in this space in neat handwriting, "I'm here to make my wife happy."

"How can I help you today?" I asked after introducing myself.

"Actually, Doctor, my wife made this appointment for me. She thinks I don't have enough interest in sex," Ted said matter-of-factly.

"Why does she think that?" I asked.

"She says it's not normal for a man to be satisfied having sex only once every month or two. At first, she wondered whether I had a mistress, but I don't, and we spend so much time together that she realizes I would need to be some kind of quick-change artist to pull it off."

"Are you satisfied having sex only once every month or two?" I asked.

"Doctor, I'm not going to tell you that our sex life is great. It's not. It's been a problem ever since I was diagnosed with diabetes three years ago, and my erections started to get soft soon after that. Alice doesn't understand that it feels stupid trying to have sex when your penis is no good anymore."

"Please tell me what you mean."

"Well, my penis never gets real hard. Ever. I can barely put it inside anymore, and that happens only if Alice gives me oral sex first. She was never crazy about oral sex through the first twenty years of our marriage, but that's the only way it's going to happen. What's even worse is that when I am finally hard enough to get inside, I come so quickly that it's like I was a teenager again."

"What about the internal hunger for sex?" I asked. "Do you feel the need to masturbate?"

"Only once in a great while," he replied.

"How about when a pretty woman walks by? Do you still notice?"

"Not the same way, Doctor. I know what you're asking, though. It used to be that I would see a good-looking woman, and I would feel a kind of electricity all through my body. But I don't get that anymore. Not at all." He then said wistfully, "That was a good feeling. I remember that. Seeing a pretty woman could brighten up my whole day!"

"Ted," I asked, "which do you remember happening first: losing the desire for sex or having trouble achieving a good erection?"

"I definitely lost the erections first," he said. "When that happened, it was like someone turned off the light switch in my head, and I've hardly had a sexual thought since then."

Ted returned to see me a couple of weeks later after completing some diagnostic studies.

"Ted," I began, "the tests show that the poor erections are due to damaged blood vessels, which is very common in men with diabetes or with other medical conditions such as hypertension or heart disease. I recommend that you try Viagra. I think there's a good chance it will help you achieve firmer erections, which should make sex more pleasurable for you and your wife."

"What about my lack of desire, Doctor? That's really what Alice was concerned about. Will Viagra help with that?"

"That's hard to say. In some men, a poor erection makes sex so distasteful to them that it is almost as if a part of their brain shuts down, and they lose their sex drive. If the erection can be improved, they start looking forward to sex again, and their desire returns. Let's see what happens to you."

"When do you suggest that I try it?" Ted asked.

"Right away! As the younger crowd says, 'Get busy, man.' Go have some fun!"

Ted smiled as he left the office holding onto his Viagra prescription.

An Unexpected Side Effect of Restored Desire

A month later, Ted returned to the office, accompanied by Alice. They were a handsome pair.

"So, Ted, what do you have to report to me?" I asked.

Ted and Alice smiled at each other like co-conspirators. Alice looked proud.

"It's been pretty good, Doctor," Ted said.

"What does 'pretty good' mean?" I asked.

"Go on, Teddy," Alice encouraged. "Tell the doctor how we've been doing since you started with the Viagra."

Ted seemed a little embarrassed. "The Viagra works well. It really does. My erection hasn't been this good in years."

I had the impression that something wasn't quite right, though. "Ted, I feel that you're holding back on me here. Is there something that isn't working out?"

"No. Not at all."

"Are you having any side effects that bother you?" I probed.

"No."

"Okay," I said, abandoning my gut feeling that there was a problem that Ted wasn't sharing with me. "Tell me, what has happened to your sexual desire?"

"Well, that's the thing, Doctor." Ted began slowly and then built up speed as he told the rest of his story. "My desire has come back like gangbusters. We've been at it nearly every night for the last couple of weeks. Alice and I haven't been like this since we first got married. And now that the children are grown and living on their own, we've taken the opportunity to inaugurate every room in the house!"

Alice blushed at this revelation.

"But I'm worried, Doctor," Ted went on.

"What's worrying you?"

"I'm afraid I'm becoming addicted to Viagra! And it's so damn expensive that it's going to eat up all our retirement money!"

The Masters and Johnson Error

When Masters and Johnson did their important work on sexual dysfunction in the 1960s and 1970s, one of their most publicized, and unfortunately incorrect, findings was that the majority of men with erection problems had a psychological basis for the problem. One reason Masters and Johnson believed this was that most of the men suffering from impotence indicated that they no longer enjoyed sex, or found it embarrassing, or avoided it, or had little desire for it any longer. Since the physical examination was normal in almost all of these men, Masters and Johnson added two and two together and confidently came up with the number three, concluding that the awkwardness regarding sex had caused the impotence. In fact, the vast majority of men with persistent erection problems have a physical basis for their problem.

One important reason that Masters and Johnson came up with their incorrect conclusion is that we have since learned that the physical changes that account for true erection problems are almost always too subtle to detect during a routine examination and instead require sophisticated tests to confirm the diagnosis. A second mistake was their belief that the negative attitudes these men exhibited toward sex was the cause of their difficulties, rather than an understandable reaction to erectile dysfunction. Men do not like having sex if they cannot feel that they are a good lover. For many men, this plays out by the brain's shutting down the desire for sex. Being able to have good sex again reawakens the sleeping lion within, and Ted was a good example. The clue in Ted's story that Viagra might prove helpful to him was that his inability to achieve a firm erection came before the loss of libido.

As we have seen, then, Viagra can indeed help some men with diminished sexual desire by helping to restore their sexual abilities. But there are many situations in which a man has lost his desire, and Viagra fails to be the solution, as we shall see in the stories to follow.

A Bad Fit

Martin was a thirty-five-year-old single man from Israel who came to see me because of trouble with erections. My secretary had warned me that Martin might be somewhat difficult to deal with, based on his gruff manner over the phone as well as when he checked in. Martin owned a software company and appeared to have done quite well for himself. He wore trendy clothes and his hair was gelled.

Martin told me that for the past nine months, his erections had been barely adequate. During this same time, he had taken up with an American woman, Cleo, who was thirty-three.

"Doctor, my penis is not working properly. I really need your help."

"Tell me what happens when you try to have sex," I asked him.

"I just told you," he replied. "My penis isn't working right."

"Is the penis firm enough to go inside?" I asked.

"Yes. But not very firm. And that is the problem."

"Does it stay firm until you have an orgasm?"

"Usually, but not always."

"What about when you masturbate? Is the penis firmer then?"

"Sometimes yes, sometimes no," he answered.

"Have you tried Viagra?"

"Yes, of course. I tried both the lower dose of 50 milligrams and the higher dose of 100 milligrams. The 100 milligram dose did seem to help somewhat."

I performed a preliminary physical examination, which showed entirely normal results, and I told Martin that we would need to do some tests to see how his penis was functioning and try to pinpoint the problem. A week later, Martin returned for his next visit.

"Martin, I'm pleased to tell you that everything checked out just fine. Your blood tests, nerve tests, the blood pressure in the penis: everything was normal. Even more important is that the results of the sleep test you took show that you achieve excellent erections while you sleep at night." I showed him the computer printout of his sleep test, revealing several erections each night with rigidity of 95 percent, some of which lasted for as long as forty-five minutes.

This was good news, of course, but Martin did not seem pleased or relieved.

"I don't understand," he said. "You're telling me that everything is fine, but I'm telling you that it's not. You don't believe me?" There was a hint of a challenge in his voice.

"Of course, I believe you," I reassured him. "All I'm telling you is that the tests show that when you are asleep and unaware that you are having an erection, your penis is able to become quite firm."

"Oh, so you think this is all in my head?" he said, stiffening in his chair.

"I wouldn't put it that way exactly," I returned. "I certainly don't mean to suggest there's something wrong with you emotionally or mentally. But sometimes the penis doesn't work properly during sex because the brain is not letting it happen. It may be because of nervousness, or depression, or problems in the relationship. Sometimes we can't even identify what happened at the very beginning of the problem, but afterward the man is so anxious about whether the penis will work properly that the blood vessels in the penis don't allow the erection to take place. The penis works best when a man looks forward to sex."

"Okay," he said. "Let's say your tests are correct. How are you going to treat me?"

"There are a number of different ways to go at this point. Some men feel encouraged just by learning that there is nothing physically wrong, and they need nothing further. Some men choose to use Viagra for a while. Still others do best by seeing a counselor or psychologist, either alone or with their partner, to explore ways to make sex more fulfilling and enjoyable."

"A psychologist!" Martin screeched. "I'm not crazy! I have no use for a psychologist!"

At this point, the telephone in the room rang, and my secretary informed me that Cleo had just arrived, late for the appointment, and wished to join us. Martin nodded his assent, and a moment later Cleo entered the room.

A Big Surprise

Cleo was all business, never bothering to apologize for being late or interrupting the conversation between Martin and me.

"So, what's wrong with Marty?" she demanded. It seemed to me that Martin had shrunk in his chair since Cleo had joined us.

"I was just giving Martin the good news that his tests show there is nothing wrong with him physically."

"That's impossible!" she said, sharply. "Marty's erections are way too soft. I don't care what your tests show! There is definitely something wrong with him."

"Martin has already told me that the penis isn't as hard as it should be when the two of you are together, but the tests show that when Martin is asleep, his penis is able to achieve excellent rigidity. Those erections occur with dreams, and since the man is unaware that his penis is erect, he cannot be nervous about them. It is really not that uncommon for a man with a normal penis to have difficulty with erections when he tries to have sex. It usually has to do with feeling nervous or awkward."

Cleo did not seem convinced. "Let's say you're right," she said, echoing Martin's response to me earlier. "What do we do about it?"

"Martin told me he had some improvement with Viagra, and I would recommend that he continue with this for the next few months. Often, men find improvement after getting themselves checked out and learning that there is nothing wrong with their equipment." I paused, wishing to avoid a repeat of the outburst that had occurred with Martin before Cleo's entrance. "Another option is to seek counseling, which is often highly successful in cases like these."

Cleo looked as if she were disgusted with both me and Martin, who sat quietly, slumped in his chair.

"What are you talking about? What do you mean Marty had 'some improvement' with Viagra? Marty and I have been together for nine months, and we've never actually had sex!"

I didn't know what to say. Had I misunderstood when I heard Martin say that Viagra had helped him? For a moment, I even wondered whether I had the wrong patient or the wrong chart.

"What do you mean?" I asked her.

"It's simple. Martin has never been able to put his penis inside me. We play around in other ways, but we've never had real sex."

"Martin, what do you have to say?" I asked.

"It's true, I suppose," he said meekly. "We have never technically had successful intercourse, although we have come close on several occasions."

"Technically?" said Cleo derisively. "We've never had sex. Why don't you just say it, Martin? Your penis doesn't get hard."

Martin shrank further in his seat.

"Martin, I don't understand," I said gently. I didn't want to put Martin too much on the spot, but I needed to know the truth if I were going to be in a position to be helpful. "If the two of you have never had sex together, then why did you tell me that the penis is hard enough to go inside?"

"My penis *is* hard enough to go in sometimes," he replied. "I'm convinced of it. It just hasn't happened yet. Often, I am firm until I am about to enter, and then it goes soft."

Cleo now turned her attention to me. "I suppose Marty hasn't told you the rest of the story either."

"The rest of the story?" I asked. Martin looked as if he wanted to escape from the room.

"Marty is a virgin. He's never had sex with *anyone*."

Martin nodded with a sheepish smile to let me know this was true.

Cleo continued, "Me? I've known a few men. Enough so that I can tell when a penis works right and when it doesn't." She paused, somewhat satisfied, as if she had set the record straight. "That's why you need to help Marty. Even if he and I don't work out, and I don't know if I have the patience to see this through, it's going to be important for him to be able to satisfy a woman someday.

"There's one more thing you should know too," Cleo added. "I think there's something wrong with his sex drive. He doesn't seem interested in sex the way a man should. We never try anything together unless I initiate it, and I'm not even sure that he tries to masturbate."

Color came to Martin's cheeks. I wasn't sure whether it was from embarrassment at Cleo's plain talk or from her criticism of his lack of desire.

Martin was in a difficult spot, and I felt badly for him. Given his outward confidence and his cool appearance, I hadn't anticipated that Martin might be a virgin. However, Cleo was a lot to handle, and it wasn't going to be easy for Martin to overcome his sexual hurdles with her. Martin needed some emotional support, and if he were to make things work out sexually with Cleo, I was certain they would need counseling.

"Okay," I said. "I'm glad that we've cleared the air. I agree with you, Cleo, that it adds to the delicacy of the situation that Martin has never had sex. A lot of men have trouble the first time."

"Yes," Cleo interrupted again, "but, Doctor, it's not as if we haven't been trying. I've got all the books. I've rented porn videos. I've even tried oral sex for him. Why didn't the Viagra work for him? Is it just a scam?"

"No, Viagra is not a scam. But sometimes the problems in a sexual relationship are too complicated for Viagra. I know Martin is opposed to it, but I really think the best chance for the two of you would be to see one of my colleagues who specializes in talking through sexual problems for couples."

"A shrink, you mean?" asked Cleo. Martin glanced warily at Cleo to see her reaction. "Listen, Marty can go if he wants. But I'm not going. This is Marty's problem, not mine." Cleo stood up suddenly. "I have another meeting to go to. C'mon, Marty, let's go."

Marty slowly rose from his seat to follow Cleo to the door. "Doctor, we'll sort it out," said Cleo. "Or maybe we won't. I don't really know." And with that she opened the door and walked out.

Martin stopped to shake my hand, saying "Thanks" as he followed her down the hall.

The Non-Viagra Solution

I was left with an empty, frustrated feeling as I watched them leave. I certainly didn't feel as if I had contributed anything worthwhile to either Martin or Cleo.

A few months later, I ran into Martin while waiting for the elevator to my health club.

"Hello, Martin," I said. "How are you?"

"Great, Doctor. Great." He smiled as we entered the elevator together. We both got off the elevator at the same floor, and he waited for everyone to disperse before he continued. "Cleo and I broke up. I have a new girlfriend now. And guess what?" He looked around to make sure there was no one within earshot. "I'm not a virgin anymore! And this girlfriend thinks I'm a sexaholic because we have sex so much!"

Relationships form for all sorts of reasons, but not all relationships are good for the people involved. It was easy to see that Martin was overwhelmed by Cleo, particularly sexually, the area where he felt most vulnerable. Presumably, both Martin and Cleo benefited in some ways from their relationship, but it was clear from their brief interactions with me that Martin was unlikely ever to find a way with Cleo where he could feel safe enough to be sexually successful. No wonder he had little sexual desire! Martin could have taken Viagra every day for twenty years, and his sex drive would never have taken hold while he was partnered with Cleo. Instead, he needed a new kind of relationship.

Depression and Desire

Sometimes lack of desire has nothing to do with hormones, or medications, or relationship issues, or erection problems. Sometimes it just has to do with the individual and how he or she is doing in life. It is hard to feel sexy when your boss is on your case, or your in-laws decide to share your tiny living quarters. As I am fond of saying to the medical students at Harvard, the mind is the largest sexual organ in the body. And if the mind is stressed, there is little room for desire.

Quinn was a fifty-two-year-old plumber who had seen me on and off for several years for a variety of minor problems. This time, he told me he was concerned because he didn't feel the same sexual urge that he once had. He had mentioned it to his buddy, who told him to see a doctor, because "it just didn't sound right to him."

I knew Quinn as a wonderful man who had taken on more than his share of caretaking in life. Three years ago, when his daughter was sixteen, she had given birth to a daughter of her own, and Quinn and his wife had taken on the parenting duties of the infant while their own daughter tried to make her way in life, working the night shift at a bakery. When Quinn and I shook hands, I had the impression that he had lost weight since his last visit.

"Tell me what's bothering you, Quinn."

"It's like all sexual feeling has left my body," he answered. "Katherine and I have been married for over twenty-five years, as you know, and we've had a good sex life together. Even when life was more like a pickle than a ham sandwich, we would still have our time together, regular-like. But now I just have no interest anymore." Quinn paused, looking for the right words. "It's like a part of me has died," he said finally.

"It looks to me as if you've lost weight too," I commented.

"You're right," he replied. "Twenty-two pounds over the last three months, and counting. I just have no appetite. Not only that, but I can't sleep either. It's a wonder I haven't messed up at work. But that's not why I came to see you, Doctor. I was wondering if you thought that Viagra might help with the sexual feeling."

"Quinn, I'm happy to talk to you about sex and Viagra in a few minutes, but right now I'm concerned about your weight loss and the difficulty you're having with sleep. Is there something going on in your life that's upsetting you these days?" I asked.

He looked directly at me, not speaking, and as I watched, the tears welled up in his eyes. Quinn's shoulders heaved as he fought the sobs that soon overtook his body. "Katherine's got cancer," he said in a loud whisper. Quinn buried his face in his large hands. I offered him a tissue, but he shook his head and instead took out his own cloth handkerchief. "It's the colon. She came through surgery beautifully, and the doctors say she's got a good chance with chemotherapy . . ." Quinn broke down again, then blew his nose and regrouped. "But I really don't know what I would do without her. How will I be able to work and still take care of my little granddaughter?"

Quinn was clearly overwhelmed and depressed. He needed support and treatment for the depression, not Viagra. Although Quinn
was able to acknowledge that he was depressed when I discussed
this with him, he had little ability to see how his depression might
have robbed him of his sexual desire.

"Why should I lose my desire?" he argued. "It's Katherine who
has the cancer, not me. She still looks great, and says it would make
her feel more normal if we had sex once in a while. She's afraid I
don't want to touch her because of her scar or because I feel sorry
for her, but it's nothing like that. I just feel dead down there."

Quinn agreed to see a psychiatrist, who successfully treated his
depression with medication. I am happy to say that Katherine
made a complete recovery after her chemotherapy, with no evidence of cancer three years following her original diagnosis.

What struck me about Quinn's story is how little he was able to
acknowledge the effects of depression and life stress on his sexual
desire. Not surprisingly, as Quinn and Katherine both recovered
from their own medical problems, their sex life returned to normal
as well.

Depression affects millions of men and women and with a wide
range of symptoms and severity. In the mildest form, a man or
woman may simply feel less vitality in life, whereas at the other end
of the spectrum, affected individuals may experience so much psy-
chic pain and hopelessness that they feel suicidal. Depression
should always be considered as a possibility when a man or woman
notices a persistent and dramatic loss of sexual desire.

Viagra and Testosterone

One of the most common reasons for a loss of sexual desire, for
both men *and* women, as it turns out, is low testosterone levels. If
this occurs, Viagra may not be helpful, since it does not address the
underlying problem. This is illustrated by Melvin and Sheila in the
following story.

Melvin was sixty-four and had been a patient of mine for nearly
ten years because of symptoms of an enlarged prostate. He always

came alone and without fail would tell me a joke before he left the office. When I walked into the examination room on this occasion, however, I was somewhat surprised to find him accompanied this time by his wife, Sheila, who was also sixty-four. Both of them were quite fit, were active tennis and golf players, and hobnobbed with the country club crowd.

"Hello, Doctor," Melvin greeted me. "Instead of a joke, today I brought you my wife," he said with a big grin. "Honey," he said turning to her, "you know I didn't mean that *you* were a joke!" he feigned concern. Sheila was used to Melvin's sense of humor.

"Hello, Doctor," she said. "I hope you don't mind that I came along today. I thought it might be helpful for me to be here too."

"Not at all," I replied. "It's a pleasure to see you. How can I be of help to both of you today?"

"Doctor, I wasn't supposed to see you until six months from now," said Melvin, "but Sheila thinks I've got a problem. She's the one who made this appointment. *I* think I'm fine. So maybe it's Sheila who has the problem," he said, winking at me.

I could tell this was going to be a sexual issue.

"Sheila, why don't you tell me what is concerning you," I offered.

"Doctor, I thought it would be a good idea to see you because our sex life has nearly disappeared," Sheila explained. "Mel had a great checkup with his primary care physician a couple of months ago, and I mentioned the same thing to him, but he just said, 'What do you expect at Mel's age?' But Mel and I are only sixty-four, and we're still extremely active and fit. It's not that Mel can't *have* sex, it's just that he never seems to be interested."

In the background, Mel was making faces and generally acting like a seven year old, as if this was all a big joke to him.

"I see," I responded. "Mel, what do you have to say about this?"

"I don't really see what the big deal is, Doctor. It's not as if we don't have sex at all. Sheila's just making a big deal out of nothing. She knows I still like ogling her."

Sheila looked upward to the ceiling in exasperation at Melvin's attempts to make sophomoric fun of the situation. "It's been going on for about two years now, Doctor," she added. "It's been a gradual thing. We used to have sex almost every week, but now we can go as long as a month or two, and then it happens only if I make a little fuss. Melvin used to be after me all the time. Not anymore, though."

"Doctor," interrupted Melvin, "please just tell her that I'm getting on in years, and we can let you be. I know you have a lot of patients waiting to see you with more important problems than this, and we shouldn't take up any more of your time. Except for a new joke I want to tell you."

"Melvin, let's be serious for just a moment," I responded. "You've told me that you find Sheila attractive. But do you still have the desire for sex like you used to? You know, that internal hunger that you once had?"

"Not like I used to, Doctor, no."

"How is your energy level these days?"

"Fine. I can't play tennis for as long as I did a couple of years ago, but I still hold my own against the younger guys."

"Do you find yourself getting tired more easily, perhaps feeling the need for an afternoon nap?"

"Funny you should mention it, Doctor. I was telling Sheila just the other day how every time I walk across my living room, I hear the couch speaking to me. Want to know what the couch says to me?"

"Sure, Melvin," I replied, playing along. "What does the couch say to you?"

"It says . . ." And here Melvin adopted a spooky voice as if he were in some grade B horror movie. "'Come to me, Melvin. Come to me and lie down.'" Melvin went back to his regular voice. "I'm taking a nap every single day now. Sometimes twice. I never did that before."

"Tell me more about what it's like when you have sex now," I asked.

"The erections are fine. But it takes more work to have an orgasm than it used to. And it doesn't feel anymore like the earth is moving. More like a whimper than a bang."

"Sheila," I said, turning to her. "Is there anything else that you'd like to add?"

"Yes, Doctor. I think Mel's a little depressed, to tell the truth. I know it's hard to tell, since he makes a joke out of everything, but he doesn't have the same spark that he once had." She took a moment and then seemed to make a decision to add something else. "It's been hard for me, Doctor. I worried initially that Mel just didn't find me attractive anymore, and that bothered me. Our children would be scandalized to hear me say this, but I've always enjoyed sex. And I've always enjoyed feeling attractive. I'm convinced now that this has more to do with Melvin than me. He just doesn't have the same pluck. Our regular doctor gave Melvin some samples of Viagra and said 'Let's see if this cheers him up,' but it didn't change anything."

An Erection in Search of Desire

Sheila left so that I could examine Mel in private, and I took the opportunity of being alone with him to ask a few more questions.

"Mel, what did you notice when you took the Viagra?" I asked.

"It was the strangest thing, Doctor. It was easier to have an erection, so that was a good thing. But there I was in the middle of having sex, and it all seemed like the oddest thing in the world to be doing what I was doing. I mean, all that grunting and groaning, sweating, the whole thing. I nearly burst out laughing because all I could think of was that my whole life I'd been chasing skirts and then trying to convince Sheila to have sex with me once we married, and I couldn't figure out why I had wasted all that time and energy on such a ridiculous activity."

Sheila rejoined us, and I told them my impression. "Melvin has classic symptoms of low testosterone," I explained. "This is common as men age, and its main symptom is diminished libido, or sex drive. Melvin has several other symptoms of low testosterone as well, such as reduced energy and possibly some mild depression. We need to confirm the diagnosis with blood tests, but if I'm right, I think there is an excellent chance that with treatment, Melvin's interest in sex will return. Even more important, Melvin will feel more vigorous in general."

Sure enough, blood tests confirmed the diagnosis of low testosterone, and Melvin started his testosterone treatment. Melvin and Sheila returned one month later to the office for follow-up.

"How are you, Melvin?" I asked.

"Doctor, the best way to put it is this. Do you remember I told you last time I was here that the sofa would call to me every time I crossed the living room? Well, the sofa doesn't call to me anymore. I've got more energy, and my tennis game is at a new level. It's like I'm twenty-five years old again!" he beamed.

"What about sex?" I asked, looking for a response from both of them.

"Oh, that!" exclaimed Melvin. "We're back to normal now. Everything is back to normal, right, Sheila?"

"Everything really *is* back to normal, Doctor," Sheila confirmed. "Melvin is back to chasing me around the house again, and it's not just to tell me some new joke, although he still does that too! We're very pleased. In fact, I was wondering if I could use a little testosterone myself."

"If you're serious about that, Sheila, we could certainly look into it," I replied. "Some women with low testosterone levels also benefit from testosterone therapy." Sheila shook her head and smiled, indicating that she was not interested.

"Doctor," Melvin spoke up, "how come Viagra didn't work for me? I thought it was supposed to be a miracle drug."

"Viagra is an effective treatment to help men with poor blood flow to the penis, but it has no direct effect on the brain, which is what controls desire," I explained. "But testosterone is a hormone that works directly on the brain, where it helps to control thoughts and feelings about sex, especially desire."

Sheila jumped in. "Mel, tell the doctor your good news."

Melvin was beaming. "Guess what?" he challenged me.

"What?" I played along again, as usual.

"I arranged to do a stand-up comedy gig at our country club next month." Melvin seemed so proud. "I've always wanted to do it, but never had the moxie to make it happen. Sheila and I would be so pleased if you would come as our guest."

Low Testosterone and Aging

Low testosterone is a topic that is gaining attention around the world. As men age, their testicles produce less and less testosterone, and it is estimated that approximately one-third of U.S. men have low levels by age sixty. The classic symptom is reduced sexual desire, but there are other symptoms as well, such as reduced energy and vitality, depressed mood, weak erections, and reduced muscle mass and strength.

There is new evidence that men with low testosterone may also be at risk for osteoporosis, just like women with low estrogen levels. Treatment can improve all of these symptoms and consists of daily treatment with a gel applied to the skin, or wearing a daily medication patch, or receiving an injection in the buttock every several weeks if the skin treatments don't work. There are some testosterone pills available, but they are not used much since they are less effective, and the ones approved for use in the United States all have the unfortunate feature of having a significant degree of liver toxicity.

Since many of the symptoms of low testosterone mimic those of normal aging and because it is so common, some in the medical profession say, "This is simply a part of the normal aging process, and we shouldn't interfere." But there are many other aspects of normal aging that greatly interfere with quality of life and are treatable. Heart disease is associated with aging, and so are arthritis, poor vision, and hearing loss. Personally, I'm glad that we have treatments for these normal accompaniments to aging, and I would like to be treated if I develop any of these.

Testosterone deficiency is really no different. Treatment restores levels to the normal range and has not been shown to cause risk of any significant medical problems. Men do need to be monitored for developing thickening of the blood and for any changes in their prostate, since there is a theoretical risk of stimulating a sleeping cancer, but so far the data are reassuring on this last count. Men who respond to treatment feel that the quality of their lives has improved. Although I would never suggest that testosterone is an antiaging medication, many men do say to me that testosterone treatment has made them feel years younger. There is much to be said for feeling vigorous and sexual again!

Learning from Viagra

Medically, there is only a short list of things that cause reduced desire in a man: medications, low testosterone, and psychological or relationship issues, for instance, depression or marital conflict. Together, these three account for approximately 90 percent of cases. Viagra helps in none of these cases, unless, as we have seen, the diminished desire has occurred as a consequence of erectile dysfunction.

The most common medications affecting desire are the antidepressants. However, there are other medications that can do this too. If a man (or woman, for that matter) notices a change in sexual desire shortly after starting a new medication of any kind, or after increasing the dosage of a medication, then it is possible that he or she is experiencing a side effect of that medication. The best thing to do in that case is to notify the prescribing physician to see if there might be alternative treatments that will not impair sexuality.

Often I am confronted by a situation in which a man in his fifties or sixties complains of diminished desire together with erectile dysfunction. In this age group, there is a good chance that he may have both low testosterone and vascular disease affecting his penis and causing the poor erections. If low testosterone is confirmed, my approach is to try testosterone first, since men who respond often feel as if they have hit a home run: everything is normal again, and there is no need to do anything special to prepare for sex, as there is with Viagra.

If the man returns and says his desire is strong again but the erections are still inadequate, I will then have him try Viagra for the erections. If this works, most men will wish to continue with testosterone too, since it makes them feel better in other ways.

There can also be a variety of reasons that a man may lose his desire without there being anything medically wrong. As we saw with Martin, this may be due to a mismatch in a relationship, or depression, or simply an awkwardness or inhibitions regarding sex. Viagra does not deal with any of this because it does not address the underlying problems. Viagra is not a treatment for depression, or for low testosterone, or for relationship issues, such as that of Martin and Cleo. Because of a lack of sophistication among many health care providers, many men complaining of poor desire receive prescriptions or samples of Viagra anyway. This stems directly from the Viagra Myth, since many men and their partners believe it is the solution to whatever ails them sexually.

The one situation where Viagra can be quite effective for diminished desire is when the erection problem came first and the part of the brain that organizes sexual thoughts becomes turned off by the idea of resuming a frustrating and embarrassing situation. Men who have experienced this may well find a return of their sexual excitement if they are once again able to be sexual with restored erections due to Viagra.

The loss of desire in a man can be a confusing issue for a woman to deal with. The stereotype, after all, is that a man is always willing and ready. If a man loses interest in sex, or never seemed to have it in the first place, it is hard for a sexual partner not to take this personally, as an indictment of her attractiveness or ability to please her man sexually.

It is only rarely the case, however, that a woman's attractiveness or bedroom skills accounts for a libido change in her male partner. More commonly, there are relationship issues that show up in the form of sexual coolness. Some men may be turned off sexually if they are angry at their partner. Or they may feel that withholding sex is the proper "punishment" for a perceived insult or injury. Men do tend to think in fairly dramatic terms. "I'll never touch her again!" is, unfortunately, a typical male response to a variety of situations.

Clearing the air by asking, "Is there something you're angry at me about?" or, "I've noticed we don't make love much anymore. Is there something bothering you?" may be useful openings to resolve conflict and to thereby restore one's sex life. Taking Viagra is unlikely to help such issues.

Lessons

- Men, and women, have a wide variation in levels of sexual desire. There is no such thing as a "normal" desire level.

- Desire varies with age and with circumstances. Stress, fatigue, an overbusy schedule, and sleep deprivation (often when there are small children in the house!) all can reduce libido.

- A change in circumstances may turn out to be the perfect cure for men with diminished desire due to "life." Many couples discover a pleasant reservoir of sexual desire during vacations when they are removed from the stresses of work and everyday life.

- Diminished desire may result from relationship issues, personal issues, depression, low testosterone levels, and as a side effect of some medications. Viagra is an ineffective treatment for all of these.

- The one circumstance where Viagra may restore desire is when the diminished libido has occurred as a result of erectile dysfunction. Allowing a man to be sexual again by improving his erection may well restore desire as well.

- Men in their fifties and beyond who notice they have developed low or absent desire should consider the possibility that they have low testosterone, especially if they also have symptoms of decreased energy and vitality and more difficulty achieving an orgasm. Low testosterone can be diagnosed with a simple blood test and is easily treatable.

- Women have an understandable tendency to view a man's lack of desire as an indication that there is something wrong with how they look or act sexually. This is rarely the case. However, there may be relationship issues that play out by a lack of desire on the part of one partner or the other. Resolving the underlying conflict will usually restore sexual interest. The simplest way to resolve problems is to talk about them.

Chapter Five

Viagra and Premature Ejaculation

Premature ejaculation is one of the most troubling sexual problems for men and their partners. Men who experience premature ejaculation worry constantly that they are failures at lovemaking and are thus inadequate sexual partners. It affects their self-esteem and their sense of sexuality and attractiveness, and it may interfere with their willingness to enter into intimate and loving relationships.

Within an existing relationship, premature ejaculation can create a major strain by making sexual contact an awkward event for both the man and the woman. Women suffer too when premature ejaculation occurs, since it short-circuits the sexual experience, leaving them feeling frustrated for themselves and uncertain how to deal with their partner's embarrassment.

It is not uncommon for a man to tell me that he is afraid his partner will leave him if I cannot help him with his quick ejaculation problem. "My wife is an attractive woman, Doctor, and I know that if I can't do a better job of satisfying her, she's going to go somewhere else." Sadly, many of these men feel so badly about themselves that they also add the following coda: "I can't say I would blame her."

As Viagra has taken over our imagination as the solution to all our sexual problems, it has also become a source of hope for men discouraged by their lack of ejaculatory control. The brilliant comedian Robin Williams does a hilarious riff in his Broadway show in which a man takes Viagra and creates sexual havoc with his never-ending erection, finally having the most mind-blowing orgasm of his life several hours later. This too is part of the Viagra Myth.

Time after time, I have had the following interaction in my office with troubled men: "Doctor, I heard that Viagra can solve my quick ejaculation," they say. "Would you prescribe it for me?"

Viagra Has No Direct Effect on Ejaculation

Unfortunately, as I explain to every man with premature ejaculation, Viagra has no direct effect on ejaculation. The impact of Viagra is quite specifically on the blood vessels of the penis, allowing greater blood flow and trapping of blood in order to augment an erection. Ejaculation, which is the expulsion of the semen, and orgasm, which is the brain and body experience of the bells and whistles that happens together with ejaculation, have more to do with nerves and muscle contractions.

Yet it is too simple to say that Viagra cannot be helpful for men with premature ejaculation. In some cases, Viagra does help by allowing men to have a second erection after they ejaculate, and possibly even a third, thus making it possible to have longer sexual contact after the first too-brief episode. Since it usually takes considerably more stimulation before an ejaculation occurs with those second and third erections, Viagra may indeed be useful in this way.

In some cases, moreover, where premature ejaculation has become part of a vicious cycle that arose initially due to sexual anxiety, Viagra may provide the confidence needed to break the cycle and thus restore a man's ability to control the timing of his orgasm. So despite not having any direct effect on the ejaculatory process, Viagra may still be beneficial for some men with premature ejaculation.

Nevertheless, for most men, Viagra is not the magic cure for premature ejaculation. As much as it is our cultural inclination to look first to our own medicine cabinet, the solution to our most vexing problems in life cannot be found there. Viagra cannot undo the behavioral training that results in so many cases of premature ejaculation, and it cannot solve the sexual anxiety or relationship issues that give rise to so many others. As a consequence, Viagra is often an unsuccessful treatment for premature ejaculation.

Whether it works depends greatly on the circumstances, as we shall see in the pages that follow.

The Emotional Impact of Premature Ejaculation

Premature ejaculation can be embarrassing and confusing for both partners.

Eloise was a divorced mother of two who related an experience with an early partner. "I was young and not very experienced sexually when it happened. I was the last one helping to clean up after a party at the home of Carl, a good friend, and soon we crossed over the friendship boundary. We started making love, but before he could even go inside me, he ejaculated. He got up from bed without saying a word and went to the bathroom. When he came out, he was dressed again. I didn't know what to say or do. I felt terrible, because it seemed it was all my fault, as if I had done something wrong. It was so awkward that I got dressed myself and left. We never really saw each other after that, and I blamed myself for a long time."

Sigmund describes the impact from a male standpoint. "I'm sixty-four years old now, and I've had a problem with premature ejaculation my whole life. It feels like a big dark secret I carry around with me. I've always been able to attract women, but when it comes to sex, I get terribly anxious because I know I'm going to disappoint them. Then I do my usual stuff to charm them to make everything okay. But if they *do* stay interested, I find myself disgusted by them, because they should have higher standards than what I can offer. It's a catch-22, I know. I've had this fantasy that if I meet the right woman and we're sexually attuned to each other, then sex will be wonderful, and I will be able to last all night, just like in the movies. But it never happens, and I think this is why I've never been able to be faithful and why my first marriage fell apart."

There is a saying in the field of human sexuality that every man wishes to see himself as the world's greatest lover. Yet how can a man conceive of himself as a good lover, let alone a great one, if the game is over before it has even begun? Katie, a young woman intent on guarding her coolness, recalled her disgust with a slightly older boyfriend who ejaculated while they were just making out in his car, soiling his pants. "Just take me home," she said to him, as if he had demonstrated so pitifully his inadequacy that she could not wait to be free of his company. "What a loser!" she exclaimed.

Early Male Sexuality

Various sources have historically labeled adolescence, especially the time around age sixteen, as the peak of male sexuality, whereas female sexuality is said to peak around age thirty. Yet any woman who has had the opportunity to engage in sexual activity with a teenage boy, and later in life with a more mature man, would surely laugh at this scientific assessment.

The good news about younger men is that their erection tends to be 100 percent firm whenever they are the least bit aroused, and they are able to have repeated erections and orgasms over a short period of time. The bad news, though, apart from simple inexperience, is that rapid ejaculation is so common.

It has now become cliché for any rite of passage movie depicting emerging male sexuality to contain some scene of embarrassed premature ejaculation. In the popular foreign film *Y Tu Mama Tambien*, two teenage male youths act out their fantasy of having sex with an older woman, who eventually chastises them both in a pique of fury because each one climaxed so quickly. "What was I thinking of," wonders the woman aloud, "taking two babies to bed with me like that."

One sexual advantage of advancing age for many men is that orgasm requires more stimulation, allowing them to have greater control over the timing of ejaculation. Mature men who may have had experiences similar to those depicted in those adolescent movies can thus look back with bemusement. Yet for some men, this problem never goes away. In other cases, it may arise as a completely new problem that rocks their sexual self.

A Lion's Pride

Although some men wonder whether their problem with quick ejaculation represents a serious physical problem, the issue is really social rather than medical. One of my favorite nature programs on television shows what happens when a new dominant male lion takes over the pride. Within the space of approximately twenty-four hours, he mates with every female in the group, meaning that he has as many as fifteen to twenty sexual encounters in that time period. This sounds like a lot of sex, but as the camera shows, each mating may take no longer than a few seconds. However, it is doubtful that any of the females would ridicule the dominant male because of the short duration of intercourse!

There are many differences between humans and lions, of course, and one of these surely is how humans have learned to separate sexuality from reproduction. When most animals mate, there is an excellent chance that a pregnancy will result. By our invention of various contraceptive methods or simply by understanding the female menstrual cycle, humans can choose whether to mate for purposes of reproduction or simply for pleasure. It is easy to calculate that approximately 99 percent of human sexual encounters in this country occur simply for the sake of having sex.

The negative aspect of quick ejaculation is its social implications: it limits the duration of the sexual encounter between man and woman. In fact, this affects the woman more than the man, because, by definition, he has already had his big release. Surprisingly, quick ejaculation isn't always a problem. Sexual pleasure and self-esteem depend so much on circumstances and expectations. What may be "too quick" in certain situations may not be too quick in others. Let me explain.

The Women's Movement and the New Sexuality

In the not-too-distant past, women were not expected to enjoy sex. Oh, sure, there were corners of enlightenment where both men *and* women explored their sexuality and where partners sought to provide each other with a pleasurable experience. But mainstream society put enormous restrictions on female sexuality.

Indeed, some of the greatest gains of feminism have been in the sexual arena. These include gaining control of one's reproductive choices with the advent of the birth control pill, promoting female awareness of one's own anatomy and function with breakthrough books such as *Our Bodies Ourselves,* and the cultural acceptance of the concept that women are entitled to as much sexual pleasure as men.

Before this, women were supposed to be virgins until they married. Sex was otherwise a deadly sin. Even within marriage, some religions taught that the only purpose of sex was for making babies. Little girls were sternly scolded for playing with their genitalia, much more than little boys were. "That's dirty, dirty, dirty," they were told. To make a baby, the man obviously needed an orgasm. But what about a woman's orgasm? It wasn't necessary and wasn't something to strive for.

It gives great insight into our cultural and historical notions of sexuality to learn that premature ejaculation was an exceedingly rare complaint to doctors prior to the advent of feminism. Why? During that time, a woman's sexuality consisted of performing her "wifely duty," meaning that as part of the marriage contract, she was expected to submit to sex with her husband. The term "submit to sex" speaks volumes about how little women were expected to enjoy the experience.

But if there was no expectation of a woman's having particular pleasure during sex, let alone reaching an orgasm, then why would anyone complain if the man ejaculated quickly? In fact, one might think that the sooner it was over, the better for both partners. Premature ejaculation became an issue only as there arose an awareness, perhaps even an obligation, for a man to try to provide pleasure for his partner and to give her at least a fighting chance to have an orgasm of her own.

Context Is Everything

How quick is too quick when it comes to the issue of ejaculation? A couple of thrusts? A minute? Two minutes? Five minutes? When I ask men and women in the office how long they think an average sexual encounter lasts once there is penetration, most answer approximately fifteen to twenty minutes. In fact, several studies have shown that humans average only a minute and a half for their sexual encounters!

This is a far cry from the idealized sex scenes in R-rated movies or erotic videos. Men tend to be enormously relieved to hear this statistic. It changes the perspective of a man who feels totally inadequate because he lasts only two or three minutes, all the while believing that his buddies are spending hours rolling around in bed with their wives or girlfriends.

Yet context *is* everything when we talk about a quick orgasm. There are many situations when a quick orgasm is desired by both the man *and* the woman. Younger couples still living with their parents or with roommates may not have the luxury of a private bedroom and an entire evening to exercise their passions. A quick sexual encounter in the basement or in the car may be just what both of them desire and need, with the speed of the event necessary to minimize the chance of detection or to reduce the odds of developing severe muscle cramps from the contortions necessary to have sex in a compact car.

Even in the more mature years, there is still the thrill of "the quickie," a brief and usually spontaneous sexual episode. The goal in these cases is the fun of just "doing it," not the idea of perfect romantic sex culminating in a simultaneous orgasm.

"I love it when Frank just *takes* me sometimes and has his way with me," explained Erica. "He gets this animal look in his eyes, lifts up my skirt, or just throws me on the bed and pulls down my pants. No foreplay, nothing. He's done in a minute, and then he goes on his way. Don't get me wrong. I wouldn't want that to be the entire extent of our sex life, but it sure adds some spice to our relationship. We both walk around with a smile the rest of the day. I never have time to come when he does that, but it makes me so hungry for him that I usually get him to take care of me later on."

Dwayne tells a story from the man's side about the value of an occasional quick ejaculation. "Luz really liked her orgasms and would get angry at me if I came too soon for her. Once, just as she was getting ready to come, I had to pull out because I felt my own orgasm coming. She was so frustrated that as soon as I was done, she wagged her finger in my face and yelled, 'Don't you ever do that to me again!'

"But another time, I took Luz on a business trip, and when we arrived at the airport, there was a limo waiting for us instead of the usual sedan. The car service that my company uses was out of sedans. Luz was all excited about the limo. After playing with the stereo and television for a few minutes, Luz slipped down and gave me oral sex. We had only a short while before the limo would drop us off. This time when I finished quickly, Luz said, 'Good boy!' to me. That trip in the limo was one of the highlights of my life." As I noted earlier, context is everything.

When Is Ejaculation Premature?

Sometimes it can be difficult to determine whether a man has premature ejaculation because there is an important variable over which he may have little control: his partner.

One day, Philip, a distinguished professor of ethics, came to see me. A vigorous man in his early fifties, he was in a second marriage and was distraught about his sexual function.

"I just can't last long enough to please my wife," he told me. "She says that I should be able to control my ejaculation better. She only rarely has an orgasm with my penis still inside her. I feel like an awful lover for her."

"Was this a problem with your first wife?" I asked.

"Not at all," he replied. "Something must have happened to me, because my first wife was able to have an orgasm nearly every time we had sex. It's such a shame, because otherwise I am so much happier and better suited with my current wife than with my first wife."

"I know you've probably never really timed it," I began, "but how long would you say it took you to ejaculate when you had sex with your first wife?"

"About five minutes," he replied.

"And how long does it take with your current wife?"

"About five minutes," he answered. And then he smiled, as if a light bulb had gone off over his head.

Philip's "performance" had been the same with both women. With one, what he offered was fine, yet with the other, it was inadequate. Philip's current wife needed more stimulation to achieve an orgasm than his first wife had. Did Philip have premature ejaculation? It all depends on one's point of view.

The Non-Viagra Solutions

Men with premature ejaculation hold themselves in contempt. Like men with erectile dysfunction due to performance anxiety, these men feel as if their body has betrayed them, and they have little control over what is going on. It is no wonder that any number of treatments and home remedies have been concocted to solve this problem.

Perhaps most amusing is the advice given to each other by teenagers and young adults. "Just think about death, man," goes one version, the idea being that thinking about something as unsexy as possible will hopefully prolong the time until ejaculation. Some young men take a different approach by biting the inside of their cheek during sex to cause themselves pain, hoping this will dampen their level of sexual arousal and thus delay orgasm.

Do these techniques work? Thinking unpleasant thoughts or causing oneself to be in pain seems contrary to the idea of sex as a pleasurable activity. Yet for many men, the goal of achieving some degree of control over their ejaculation is so important that it makes this a fair trade-off.

In the movie comedy *There's Something About Mary*, a young man is given advice by his more experienced friend before going on a date with his beautiful dream girl. "You can't go out there with a loaded gun," he's told, meaning that he should masturbate before the date so that his excitement is reduced to a manageable level.

Many men have used this strategy to help them with premature ejaculation. They masturbate before they have sex with their partner, since after each orgasm it takes more and more stimulation to climax again. When sex occurs, they are able to last longer with their partner and thus feel like a better lover.

Women are usually shocked to hear this. "Ugh! That's disgusting! Why does he need to masturbate before he has sex with me?" The whole thing sounds unnatural to women and hard to accept. Men who practice this may not be particularly happy about it either, but they gladly accept it if it works for them, since nearly anything seems better than suffering the humiliation of the overly quick ejaculation.

A more palatable variation for some couples is to accept a quick initial ejaculation by the man, followed by longer-lasting sex when he regains an erection. The man thus has more than one orgasm, and the woman should have a greater opportunity the next time around to have her own satisfaction. However, this doesn't work if the man has trouble achieving a second erection in a reasonable period of time, or if the man or woman feels that this pattern does not follow the script that they keep in their minds as to what constitutes "normal" sex.

Other common "home" treatments include using one or more condoms at a time in order to decrease sensation in the penis or to even use creams or sprays to anesthetize the penis.

The Classic Treatment

Before Viagra, the classic treatment for men with premature ejaculation was called biosensate therapy in combination with the "choke technique." In this treatment, men would engage in sexual play, either by themselves or preferably with a partner, and would try to learn the various stages of their own body's arousal. A few moments before orgasm occurs for a man, there is a "point of inevitability" when an orgasm is going to occur, even if there is no more direct stimulation of any kind.

The challenge is for the man to be able to identify when he is approaching the point of inevitability and without crossing over that line. If he can do so, then in theory he can stop thrusting at that point, thus deferring ejaculation. As a rule, the feeling of an impending ejaculation will subside after a few moments without stimulation, and then sexual activity can resume. This pattern can be repeated over and over again, giving the man control over when he will ejaculate.

Often, especially at the beginning, it is difficult to distinguish when one is approaching the point of inevitability, and ejaculation occurs even if the man tries desperately to stop all stimulation. But sometimes it is possible to abort the oncoming ejaculation by grabbing the penis and squeezing it hard. This is called the *choke technique*. The erection may disappear with this maneuver, but it usually reappears shortly with continued sexual activity.

Biosensate therapy works well but requires practice and commitment. It may not be a viable option for some men, though, because it is difficult to do without a stable relationship and a willing partner. Although it is possible to "go into training" on one's own, sex just isn't the same without a partner. Biosensate therapy also may not be appropriate with a new relationship, because it takes time to develop the level of commitment and trust needed to ask a partner to become involved in sex therapy. Nevertheless, learning to control one's ejaculation can be a major life-enhancing event for men who choose this path.

One of the more recent and effective treatments has been the use of the serotonin reuptake inhibitors, which are most commonly prescribed for depression. These medications cause delayed ejaculation in many men. This can be an annoying side effect for men who take this type of medication for depression or anxiety, but it can be an excellent treatment for the man with premature ejaculation. Some of my patients have success by taking the medication only when they are about to have sex, whereas others require a small daily dose, even on days when they do not intend to have intercourse.

One drawback of this treatment is that the quick ejaculation usually returns once the man stops taking the medication. In contrast, once a man learns to control his ejaculation, the benefits last forever.

The Male Imperative to Please

One of the themes that informs male sexuality is the male imperative to please his partner. I know this runs counter to the stereotype of the thoughtless clod of a man who is nearly oblivious of his female partner and her sensibilities and concerns as he runs through life like a bull in a china shop. Yet it is a common issue that men bring up when they speak with me privately in the office and a common reason why men ask for Viagra.

"He barely notices when I cut my hair," or "He just won't listen when I try to tell him about my problems," may be common female complaints, and true, but it's not fair to boil down certain gender differences to the generalized complaint that men are uninterested in their partners. My experience with men is that as a rule, they are painfully desirous of being able to please their women. This plays out especially in the realm of sex.

Men enjoy being useful. They function well when the goals are clear, in which case they can set their sights, put their heads down, and plug away at whatever challenge is in front of them. This is true in relationships, and it is true in sex. Unfortunately, as we saw in Chapter Three on performance anxiety, sex can be a difficult area in which to simply work harder if things are not working out.

There is clearly a psychological component to this too, as exemplified by Colin. "Doctor, I can have an erection all day without ejaculating if I'm just fooling around with my girlfriend. She can go down on me, touch me, everything. But the instant my penis goes inside her vagina, it's all over. It's like I have no control over it. I don't understand it." There's something about entering the woman—the warmth of the vagina, the embrace and closeness that usually accompanies face-to-face penetration—that makes some men have an immediate orgasm.

Quick ejaculation may be a trained behavior. Many young people have their early sexual experiences where there is fear of discovery, such as in the basement while the parents are upstairs or in a car. Simply "doing it" becomes the goal, and quick ejaculation may not be seen as a problem under those circumstances. This may turn out to be a trained behavior that is difficult to break later, though, when there is an opportunity for more relaxed lovemaking.

Let's now take a look at when Viagra can help premature ejaculation and when it can't.

A Viagra Success

Nick was a forty-two-year-old Greek engineer who wrote on his medical form that his reason for seeing me was, "My wife is going to leave me." When I stepped into the exam room, Nick smiled quickly, and when I offered my hand to say hello, he grabbed it in both of his own and held it without letting go for a few moments. "Doctor, thank you for seeing me. I am desperate for your help."

"What seems to be the problem?" I asked.

"My entire life is falling apart," he began. "I've been married to Elena for twenty-two years. We have three grown boys. We've had a good life together." He smiled weakly. "And now, Elena says she is going to leave me." Nick started shaking, a little overdramatically.

"Why did she say that?" I asked.

"Two months ago, Elena tells me that in all the years we've been together, she's never had an orgasm. Not once." Nick's mouth turned downward, and his lower lip pouted out as he tried to hold himself together. "I couldn't believe it. I never knew. All this time, I thought she was satisfied with me. She tells me I ejaculate too quickly for her. If I don't get any help, she says she's going to leave me. She says that it is only right that she has some pleasure with sex too."

Nick crossed his arms, looking as if he wanted to hold himself. "All my life I thought I was a good husband, and now I find out I'm a failure!" he exclaimed.

"Tell me what happens when you and Elena have sex together," I asked.

"I thought everything was fine," he said. "I get hard, I put my penis inside her, and I finish. Elena tells me now that it's too quick. She always made sounds like she was enjoying it. How was I supposed to know that it's been no good for her?"

"How long does it take before you have an ejaculation?"

"I come right away, Doctor. Twenty seconds, thirty."

"Has it always been this way, Nick?"

"Doctor, Elena is the only woman I've ever been with. We've been having sex the same way our entire lives. It was good enough to have three strong boys, but now it's not. Of course, I see she should have some pleasure. I just never thought about it before, and now it's the only thing I think about."

"What have you tried to do so far to help yourself?"

"My friends told me about this stuff in the drugstore, so I tried it. It's a spray. It makes the penis cold, and it says it's supposed to reduce the feeling. But it didn't work for me, and I felt stupid with it."

"Do you ever try to give Elena pleasure by touching her down below with your hand or with your mouth?

"Doctor, I've tried that since she gave me the big news. But it's not something we're used to doing, and even talking about it feels strange."

We talked more, and in the end I thought it would be worthwhile for Nick to try Viagra. I explained that Viagra did not work directly on the ejaculatory process and would not necessarily slow down his initial ejaculation, but it might make it easier for him to have another longer-lasting erection, which might be nice for Elena. We also talked about introducing some foreplay into their sex life. Some women can reach an orgasm even if the man comes quickly as long as she is highly aroused by the time the penis is inserted. Nick thanked me and trotted down the hall with new enthusiasm.

Nick showed up for the next visit with Elena by his side. "Doctor, I didn't take the Viagra. Elena wanted to talk to you first."

Elena was a little plump and exuded a healthy vitality. She wore bright red lipstick and showed off her ample cleavage with a tight top.

"Doctor, I've been a good wife and a good mother. I never asked for anything for myself. But now that my boys are grown and out of the house, I don't think it's so terrible for me to ask for a little something for myself. Tell me, is it so terrible?"

I smiled and shook my head, encouraging her to go on.

"I picked up a book at the all-female gym I go to and started reading about my body. I haven't told Nick about this yet, but he may as well hear it. The book showed me how to touch myself, and I had my first orgasm ever. By myself." Nick looked on incredulously, while Elena proudly sat up in her chair as she continued. "I want to have that feeling while I'm having sex with my husband, like other women do."

Nick cast his eyes downward, shamed.

"Elena, I think it is great that you've been able to discover your sexuality," I said. "The challenge now is to figure out how to make this a positive part of your marriage. I wonder if there's a way for the two of you to have fun together in your sex life."

"Do you think that's possible?" she asked doubtfully. "Nick is so depressed these days. It's as if I had told him I wanted to get divorced."

"Actually," I said, looking over at Nick, who remained silent and avoided my eyes, "Nick told me that you were going to leave him if he couldn't solve his problem with quick ejaculation."

Elena's eyes twinkled. "Nicky gets carried away sometimes, Doctor. I did tell him that some women leave their husbands if they can't satisfy them. But I have no intention of leaving Nicky. I still want him to be able to last longer with sex, though, so I can have an orgasm every now and then."

I explained to Elena, as I had to Nick, that Viagra did not directly affect the time to ejaculation, but could help Nick achieve a second erection after he climaxed.

"What this means, Elena, is that Nick might finish just as quickly as he did before, but then he might be able to have another erection. If he does, that next erection almost always lasts longer. Shall we try it?"

They both agreed, and I gave Nick a prescription.

The Joy of Sex

Nick and Elena returned to visit me two months later. They seemed as if they shared some great secret, and Nick carried a bag from bookseller Barnes and Noble close to his chest as if it contained a precious cargo. Their body language told me that things were going well, and I was touched by the idea that they had brought me a gift. Elena had lost a few pounds, and curiously, Nick looked as if he had put on some weight, which suited him fine.

"Elena and I are doing really well now," Nick said with obvious satisfaction. "I still finish quickly with the Viagra, but then I get hard again. Elena thinks it's a miracle. And sometimes I last a long time even without Viagra! We've even started to go to bed early now, Doctor, so that we have more time for our new hobby together!"

The two of them clasped hands and giggled together like naughty schoolchildren.

"We're so very grateful, Doctor," said Elena. "We feel like we have a new world to explore together. All this time, we've been just doing the same thing, over and over, and neither one of us really had a chance to enjoy our bodies or each other." She motioned to Nick to bring out the contents of the bag. "We've brought you something . . . ," at which point Nick pulled a book from the bag, and I prepared to thank them for their thoughtfulness, ". . . to sign for us. Will you?" she asked. The book was *The Joy of Sex*, a popular sex manual. The gift wasn't for me, but for them!

"Of course," I replied, laughing at myself, and wrote inside the front cover that I wished them a lifetime of sexual enjoyment and intimacy. Elena took the book from me and read this aloud with satisfaction to Nick. He leaned over to give Elena a kiss on the cheek, winked at me, and led her out the door.

Although the book was not for me, Nick and Elena had indeed given me a gift. It is inspiring to witness men and women breaking through years of cultural training to find new and more satisfying ways to relate to each other.

There is a saying that "when one is finally ready for change, growth happens quickly." Nick and Elena had bridged a first obstacle, and with the help of Viagra they had journeyed far beyond where they or I had anticipated them traveling, on the road to sexual self-expression.

A Viagra Failure

Sometimes premature ejaculation occurs as a result of issues within a relationship. Viagra is less likely to be effective in these situations, since there is no way for Viagra to help solve the underlying relationship problems.

"I'm going crazy with Felicia," began Ahmed, a thirty-three-year-old consultant for a large software company. "She expects me to be able to read her mind! I can tell within ten seconds of coming home that she's upset about something, but she refuses to tell me what it is. So I have to start playing the game of twenty questions, like, 'Is it something I did, or something that I didn't do?' But she'll never answer directly. Instead, she'll make me even more frustrated by saying 'If you have to ask, then maybe we don't belong together.' So I start reviewing in my head all the things that I did and didn't do since the last time she seemed okay with me.

"Just the other day I came home from work, and I could instantly tell she was pissed off at me. 'What's wrong?' I asked.

"'Nothing,' she answers.

"'Come on, tell me,' I say as nice as I can. 'I can tell you're upset. Just tell me what it is.'

"'Forget about it,' she says. Finally after half an hour of probing and cajoling, it turns out that when I left the house in the morning, I hadn't wished her good luck on a presentation she was making that day. I also didn't call her during the day to ask about it, and then I made everything worse by not asking about it the moment I stepped into the house."

Sex Imitates Life

"What does this have to do with your sex life?" I asked.

"*What* sex life?" he asked sarcastically. "We rarely have sex anymore. Felicia gets pissed off at me with sex too, and it's just not worth it. We've been together for two years now, and we were getting by all right until about six months ago. One night, I came home exhausted from a business trip, but we wound up having sex that night anyway. I came almost as soon as my penis went inside.

"Felicia acted as if I had done it on purpose, as if I wanted to get it all over with so I could just roll over and go to sleep. She accused me of being inconsiderate of her feelings and sexual needs. It became this thing that was so much larger than sex. According to Felicia, my inability to hold off on my orgasm was symptomatic of our whole relationship and showed how little I valued her."

"And then what happened?"

"We eventually made up, but the next few times we had sex, I came right away again. The more I tried to hold back, the quicker I came. 'Premature ejaculation' I guess you'd call it. Felicia would give me that look, the one that says, 'See. All you really care about is you.' She acted as if I had control over it, but I don't!"

"What's this like for you?" I asked.

"It makes me feel alone and hopeless."

"Do you mean hopeless about sex?"

"With everything in the relationship, not just the sex. No matter what I do, all she sees is that I'm selfish and inconsiderate. It used to be that our best and closest moments were in bed together, but now sex is a disaster. I was hoping that Viagra could take care of the sex part, and maybe then we'll find our way back to each other."

After discussing the various treatment choices, Ahmed wanted to try Viagra. I wasn't sure that this was a situation where Viagra would be effective, but it was worth a try. Ahmed promised to return in two months, bringing along Felicia if she were willing.

Viagra Fails to Solve Underlying Issues

Ahmed did indeed return, but not with Felicia. "How did it go?" I asked.

"Viagra didn't help," he answered. "I was able to get hard again soon after I came, but ejaculation was still very quick. Once after I took Viagra, I became hard again only a few minutes later. I was ready to have another try, but Felicia was already pissed off at me, and there was no way she was going to let me touch her by then." He clucked as if he were stumped by a math problem. "Why didn't Viagra work?" he asked.

"Quick ejaculation can result from anxiety, and I was hoping that Viagra would give you enough sexual confidence to allow you to control your ejaculation better," I explained. "But there is so much conflict and unresolved issues between you and Felicia that it's not that big a surprise that Viagra didn't work."

"What's the answer, then?" he asked.

"I see two issues here, Ahmed. The first is that you and Felicia have a pattern of relating that has you constantly on edge. And the second is that sex has stopped being something that you enjoy with Felicia. Instead of being able to lose yourself in passion and pleasurable feelings, you're busy thinking about avoiding ejaculation. There can't be much to look forward to in *that*!"

"So what do we do?"

"I think you and Felicia need an opportunity to work on your relationship. The best chance for the two of you to get back on track is by bringing the issues out into the open with a skilled therapist who can defuse the anger and give each of you a chance to feel positively about each other again."

"Felicia would never agree to see a counselor, Doctor. We tried it once, and she swore she would never do that again. Either I loved her the way she was, or it was just too bad."

"Why don't you bring her here, then, to talk about the sexual part of things, and we'll see where we get to," I suggested.

A Woman's Perspective on Premature Ejaculation

The following week, Ahmed and Felicia were waiting for me in the consultation room. Felicia, a pretty woman in her early thirties dressed in a smart business suit, seemed quite comfortable being there.

"Hello, Felicia," I began. "Ahmed has told me about the sexual problems he's been having, and it's great that you could join us today."

"I'm relieved you called it 'Ahmed's problem,'" Felicia said. "When Ahmed first asked me to come here, I was certain that he was going to blame his problem on me too."

"Are there other things that Ahmed blames you for?" I asked.

"Just about everything!" she exclaimed. "He says I'm the source of all tension and stress in his life. If you were to believe everything that Ahmed says, I'm even responsible for global warming!"

Ahmed looked as if he wanted to object, but he kept silent.

I smiled at the last comment. "From your point of view, Felicia, what seems to be the problem?"

"Our sex life is a big waste of time, Doctor. Ahmed ejaculates almost as soon as he enters me. I don't know why he does that, but it sure doesn't make me want to have sex!"

"What's it like for you, Felicia?"

"It's frustrating. I *like* sex. I like the buildup, I love it when I have an orgasm, and I enjoy the feeling afterward too. Ahmed and I used to have a *great* sex life. But it's all a big letdown now. When he comes so quickly, it's like, 'Why even bother?' There's nothing in it for me."

The Big Yank

"Are these new feelings for you, Felicia?"

"Doctor, our sex life had soured before this latest problem crept into our lives. Ahmed doesn't seem to care about anything during sex except his own pleasure."

"Why do you say that?" I asked.

"Take oral sex, for example. It's been ages since Ahmed went down me. Yet he still wants me to do it for him."

"That's not fair, Felicia," interjected Ahmed. "I've tried several times over the last couple of months to go down on you, and you always give me the big yank."

"The big yank?" I inquired.

"Yeah," replied Ahmed. "I'll be down there trying to please her, and within moments, I feel her pulling on my hair to bring my head back up. It's not that I don't *want* to do it; it's that she won't *let* me. I guess I don't do it right for her."

"That's not it, Ahmed," corrected Felicia. "I know you don't want to be doing it. And I don't want you going down on me because you think you're supposed to. I don't need any favors from you."

"How do you know whether I want to be doing it?" he asked.

"Because you're never hard when you're going down on me!" Felicia exclaimed loudly.

"But that's because you have me so worried whether I'm doing it right!" Ahmed responded, also with raised voice. "I'm busy wondering how many nanoseconds you'll let me stay down there before you yank me back up again by my hair."

Felicia and Ahmed glared at each other, panting heavily like bulls about to face off against each other.

This seemed a good time for me to intervene. "Let me stop you guys for a moment and tell you what I hear. Felicia, I hear that you don't believe that Ahmed cares about you and your feelings as much as you'd like, and that when he does something for you, you think it's because he feels obligated rather than because he truly wants to. Is that about right?" Felicia nodded.

"And Ahmed, I hear that you feel as if Felicia doesn't appreciate what you do to try to please her, and you end up feeling confused. Does that sound about right?" He nodded. "I suspect this plays out in other parts of your relationship too, not just with sex. Is that right?" They both nodded.

Felicia grinned and looked at Ahmed, who also broke into a half-smile.

"Why are you smiling?" I asked.

Felicia answered. "It's funny to hear it described so simply. I *love* Ahmed. I really do. But we get into these catfights that never seem to end. One of us is always angry at the other."

Finding a Romantic Solution

"Let's see if we can't find a way to turn this into something positive for both of you," I proposed. "Ahmed, what would you like to see happen more than anything else in your sex life with Felicia?"

"I'd like to feel that I'm the best lover Felicia's ever had," he responded without hesitation. "I'd like to be able to give her incredible pleasure."

Felicia listened with a skeptical look on her face.

"Felicia, what's your fantasy of what you'd like in your sex life with Ahmed?"

"I'd like to feel pampered and spoiled by Ahmed as if I were some beautiful princess," she said with a faraway look in her eyes.

"Perfect!" I exclaimed. "It sounds to me as if both of you want the same thing, so why don't we make it happen." Ahmed and Felicia looked at me in puzzlement. "Ahmed wants to please you,

Felicia, and you want him to please you. It's a perfect fit. Here's what I want you to do. Sometime in the next week, you should set aside an evening. Ahmed's job is to do everything he can to make you feel like that princess. Do whatever comes into your head, Ahmed—oils, scents, candles, whatever. Be creative, and have fun with it."

Felicia was smiling with the thought of being pampered, as Ahmed listened intently. "But that evening is only about Felicia. In fact, Ahmed, you are not *allowed* to put your penis inside Felicia that night or to request or expect any sexual attention from her whatsoever. The goal is for you to be able to shower Felicia with all the attention that she craves and that she deserves from her lover." Felicia clearly liked this last part of the instructions. "Can you do it, Ahmed?"

"Absolutely. It sounds like a lot of fun!" he replied enthusiastically. "I've got some ideas already!"

"As for you, Felicia, your job is simpler but not necessarily easier." Both Felicia and Ahmed were sitting forward now in their chairs. "Your job is to *allow* Ahmed to please you. You must promise to let go of any thoughts that he is fulfilling some obligation, and be open to the idea that he wishes to actively love you and that you are entitled to experience his love as a gift."

"Doctor," Felicia interrupted, "it doesn't seem quite fair for me to get all that attention. What about Ahmed?"

"Here is the piece to understand that can propel both of you to a better place of being with each other. By letting Ahmed love you and letting him know that you appreciate his love, you are giving him a precious gift as well."

Felicia sat back in her chair and suddenly brought her hands up to her face as if she'd been slapped. Ahmed watched her silently. "I get it," she said after a moment. "I just need to let Ahmed love me."

Felicia started to get up, but Ahmed stopped her. "Doctor, this all sounds great, but what does this have to do with my premature ejaculation?" he asked.

"Nothing and everything," I answered. "If you guys can do what I suggested for even one night, I think the ejaculation problem will solve itself. In fact, I think it may have been solved already."

Ahmed seemed a little unsure, but Felicia understood. Ahmed's quick ejaculation came from his anxiety about lovemaking with Felicia. By offering Ahmed her acceptance of his love, Felicia knew that his anxiety would disappear, and his poor ejaculatory control would vanish at the same time.

I didn't hear from Ahmed and Felicia again for more than a year. One April day I received a card in the mail. There was a wedding picture of the two of them inside and a note from Felicia.

"Dear Dr. M.," she wrote. "As you predicted, the problem for which we consulted you was solved by the time we left your office. With your help, Ahmed and I have found a wonderful home in each other. Now, we're building an addition of sorts, in order to accommodate all the joy and fullness in our lives. Baby Joshua or Baby Jasmine (we don't want to know the sex yet!) is expected to join us sometime this summer. Thank you so much for helping us open our eyes, and our bodies, to each other."

Learning from Viagra

The Viagra Myth fails men and women when they expect a pill to solve complex relationship issues or to alter their ingrained ways of behaving. With premature ejaculation, Viagra can sometimes be helpful in indirect ways, but success depends greatly on individual circumstances.

Premature ejaculation causes enormous sexual difficulties for both the man and his partner. A quick ejaculation makes a man feel like a bad lover and makes it difficult for the woman to have enough time to have much pleasure or to reach an orgasm. Quick ejaculation conflicts with the romantic images we carry in our heads about what constitutes good lovemaking and does not permit enough time for a coherent, passionate expression of our feelings for each other.

On a practical level, it is difficult for both the man and the woman to know what to do about the situation. As we saw with Ahmed, the harder a man tries to delay his orgasm, the more anxious he becomes, which makes it even more likely that he will climax rapidly. Women may find it challenging to be supportive of their partner when they are unable to find much pleasure in sex for themselves. "At least he gets to have an orgasm," is a complaint, spoken or unspoken, of many women.

Nick was devastated when he learned that Elena had never had an orgasm with him. It violated his concept of himself as a good husband and as a man. Elena's desire to have Nick be more amorous and long-lasting created difficulties for Nick because his tendency to ejaculate quickly was ingrained. Viagra gave Nick a second chance to be a good lover for Elena, not by delaying the ejaculation itself but by allowing him to continue with sexual activity even after the first orgasm.

Viagra was ineffective for Ahmed because his rapid ejaculation was due to his complex relationship with Felicia rather than a long-standing behavioral pattern. Once the relationship improved, the premature ejaculation disappeared. Not all sexual problems are helped by increasing blood flow to the penis.

Addressing the sexual problems in a relationship offers an opportunity to open up a world of possibilities for couples that they might never have otherwise envisioned.

Lessons

- It is rare for sex to be as ideal as the images we see in movies or read about in books. One of the most common reasons that our own sexual experiences do not measure up to those ideals is premature ejaculation.

- Premature ejaculation can be devastating to a man because of his wish to provide pleasure to his partner.

The role of pleasure provider is critical to a man's sexual self-image. Premature ejaculation interferes with this because it makes it impossible for a man to see himself as a successful sexual being.

- Women suffer too when their partners experience premature ejaculation. Sex becomes frustrating and disappointing.

- Viagra has no direct effect on the process of ejaculation, but it can be helpful for some men with premature ejaculation. Viagra allows many men to have a second or even third erection, which makes it possible to prolong the sexual encounter. It also can increase a man's confidence in his sexual prowess, thereby eliminating the anxiety that leads to some cases of rapid ejaculation.

- Viagra is likely to be ineffective for premature ejaculation if there are complex relationship issues that have contributed to the problem.

- A number of non-Viagra treatments for premature ejaculation are available. The classic treatment is biosensate therapy, in which the man learns how to adjust the level of stimulation during sex according to his degree of arousal.

- Serotonin reuptake inhibitor medications are an effective treatment for many men with premature ejaculation. These medications work by delaying the time until orgasm. However, the problem generally recurs if the medication is discontinued, because the medication does not deal with the underlying behavioral, anxiety, or relationship issues.

Chapter Six

When Viagra Doesn't Work

It would be wonderful if Viagra worked every time, for every man with an erection problem. Unfortunately, this is not the case. But this is not a deficiency of Viagra, which is an excellent medication, and a true advance in the field of sexual medicine.

This notion of Viagra as an automatic solution, as the quick fix to all sexual problems, reflects our society's tendency to simplify the struggles that are part of life, and this assumption that Viagra will always work is also part of the Viagra myth. We break things down into good and evil, black and white. We create unrealistic expectations, and can then be severely disappointed if those expectations are not met.

As great as this medication may be, the reality is that approximately a third of men who try Viagra for erection problems will not find it successful. Another large segment may find that it is not what they expected or what they would like. Data show that less than 50 percent of U.S. men refill their Viagra prescriptions. For every man who feels as if he's scored a touchdown when he takes Viagra for the first time, there is another man who is puzzled by the fact that Viagra did not work for him. "I guess all that great stuff I heard about Viagra was just another case of hype," these disappointed men say to me in the office. "What a piece of junk!"

The Viagra Myth makes us lose sight of the complexity of relationships, sexuality, and health. Viagra is neither panacea nor junk. Not surprisingly, the effectiveness of Viagra is closely related to the severity of the sexual problem and the medical condition of the man taking it.

Overcoming Inflated Expectations

Some of the mythology around Viagra results from the early medical literature. Perhaps the most important one was a study that appeared in 1998 in the renowned *New England Journal of Medicine*. In that study, Viagra was reported to work in 80 percent of men who tried it at the full dose of 100 milligrams. In medicine, anything that works 80 percent of the time is phenomenal, and this is the way those results were reported in the newspapers.

However, in that same study, 40 percent of men who took a placebo pill also thought their treatment was a success. This too was a very high number. Does the high success rate for placebo mean that men with erectile dysfunction have primarily a psychological cause for their problem, since they seem to be so susceptible to cure with a sugar pill? Does Viagra work mainly by being a placebo?

As with many other studies, the answers lie in the details. How men are selected for a study will determine to a great extent the type of results that are possible. The high percentage of success with placebo means that the group of men who were studied contained a large number of men who had psychological issues contributing to, or causing, their erectile dysfunction. Viagra did indeed work very well for this group. But the success rate would certainly have been less impressive if there had been more men with a physical cause for their erectile dysfunction.

Over the past several years, we have learned a great deal about the success of Viagra, based on numerous studies in different population groups. We now know that Viagra works in about two-thirds of men overall. Success rates are best in men with performance anxiety or other forms of psychogenic impotence and are lower, perhaps no more than 50 percent, in men with complicated medical conditions that include diabetes and heart disease.

Some men hear that there is only the 50 percent success rate for their condition, and they become discouraged. However, I personally think it is an outstanding number. For most of the years I was treating erectile dysfunction prior to the development of

Viagra, I thought it would be impossible to develop an effective and safe drug. How could a pill be designed that would affect the blood vessels in the penis without causing disastrous effects in the rest of the body? Yet this is exactly what Viagra offers us, due to its action on a specific enzyme found almost exclusively in the smooth muscle inside the penis.

To have a pill that works in half of the men with difficult cases of erectile dysfunction is not a bad result. Fortunately, there are more options for treating men with erectile dysfunction than Viagra alone. In fact, our treatments are so successful that my colleague Irwin Goldstein at Boston University Medical School, an internationally recognized leader in the field of sexual medicine, is fond of saying, "If you own a penis, we can give you an erection."

How an Erection Works, and Why It Fails

When a man achieves an erection, a staggeringly complex set of events has taken place. The brain sends signals through nerves to the blood vessels of the penis to fill the penile chambers with blood from the arteries. At the same time, there is relaxation of the smooth muscle fibers within the chambers to hold the blood, and the outflow tracts via the veins are shut off to trap the blood within the penis. Arousal requires the brain to distill all the subtle signals in the environment—touch, smell, sight, sounds—and is governed by hormones, especially testosterone in men.

Because erections depend on so many systems—arteries, veins, nerves, hormones, brain—it means that they are also vulnerable to problems. Indeed, if any one of the erection components fails, then erections fail as well. All cylinders must be hitting for the man to get a rise in the desired location.

Some of the more common medical conditions that cause impotence are hypertension, diabetes, heart disease, and high cholesterol. Smoking and alcohol can contribute to erectile dysfunction as well. Nerve problems from multiple sclerosis, spinal cord injury, or pelvic surgery, such as for prostate cancer, can cause erection problems, since the nerves are what tells the blood vessels in the penis to create the erection.

The more of these risk factors that a man has, the more likely he is to have difficulties with erections. And the more severely the penis has been affected, the less likely it is that Viagra will work. Many men with these conditions have already tried Viagra and found that it didn't work for them.

It is a shame that so many men who fail with Viagra give up altogether on their sex lives, since what Dr. Goldstein says is true: almost any man can find a treatment that will allow him to have sex again. But many people are unaware that treatments other than Viagra exist or that they can be effective. Our emphasis on Viagra has made us blind to the variety of other treatments that are available.

Alternatives to Viagra

Although it surprises many people to hear this, the treatment of erectile dysfunction was quite effective before Viagra was even a glimmer of possibility. The limiting factor, and the reason most people didn't know about any of it, was that there was no pill to offer, so none of the treatments captured anyone's attention.

Viagra's claim to fame, and it will likely always be thus, is that it was the first *oral* medication for erectile dysfunction that worked. No matter how many other variations on Viagra or other types of pills arrive on the market in the years to come, Viagra will be seen as a major event in the history of medicine and the pharmaceutical industry.

The most common treatment for men who fail Viagra, or who can't take it because they also take nitrate medication, the combination of which can produce dangerous side effects, is penile injection therapy, which has been around for twenty years. As with other events in the history of the treatment of erectile dysfunction, it's a wonderful story.

Penile Injection

The time was 1983, and at the annual meeting of the American Urological Association in, of all places, Las Vegas, there was scheduled a presentation by a maverick physiologist from Britain named Giles Brindley.

Brindley was known for interesting experiments and results, and wasn't averse to trying things out on himself. This was the same man, after all, who had surgically implanted a thermometer within his own scrotum in order to do an experiment in which he monitored the temperature around the testicles continuously for twenty-four hours so that he could learn about the relationship between temperature and the testicles. The audience was prepared for something interesting. They weren't disappointed.

Most speakers at these medical meetings wear a suit and tie and do their utmost to appear dignified and proper, all the better to support whatever new data they hope to present to their skeptical community of professors, researchers, and colleagues. Dr. Brindley showed up wearing sweatpants.

The title of Dr. Brindley's presentation offered little sense of drama. Yet the presentation was anything but boring.

Dr. Brindley began, "Ladies and Gentlemen, members and guests, thank you for allowing me the opportunity to present to you my research today. Approximately fifteen minutes ago I injected my right corpus cavernosum [the erectile chamber of the penis] with 30 milligrams of phenoxybenzamine [a medication that acts on the blood vessels]. Please note that I currently have no feelings of sexual arousal."

And with that, he stepped out from behind the podium, dropped his sweatpants, and stood there, *in flagrante*, with a full erection! He then proceeded to walk up and down the aisle so that his colleagues could get a better look and make sure that he wasn't fooling them with a penile prosthesis. Although I wasn't there to see this piece of urological theater, colleagues who did attend the meeting describe a scene of disbelief and amazement unlike anything they had ever witnessed in their medical careers. The era of penile injections had arrived with a clamor.

Penile injection therapy ushered in a new era because for the first time, there was a treatment less invasive than surgery for men with erectile dysfunction. In addition, it gave researchers a way to study erections with the penis "activated," without requiring subjects to try to be aroused while they were poked and prodded and tested by scientists. Thanks to penile injection therapy, we have learned about how erections work and how they fail. Instead of the hemodynamics used to describe the study of how the heart and blood vessels work, we now had something we call, tongue-in-cheek, "peno-dynamics."

Although most men cringe at the thought of putting a needle anywhere near their penis, it turns out to be a relatively easy and almost completely painless thing to do. The needles are tiny, and men who give themselves shots for other reasons, most commonly diabetics giving themselves insulin, say that this injection is less bothersome.

Injections have some advantages. When Viagra came out, nearly every one of my injection patients wanted to try it, of course. I was surprised when some of these men chose to continue with injections, even though they had success with Viagra.

"Injections are more spontaneous for me," explained Sid, a forty-eight-year-old diabetic who had been using injections for three years with good success. "I know it sounds funny to say that a needle is more spontaneous than a pill, but my wife thinks sex shouldn't be planned. The needle gets me hard within a few minutes, and it doesn't matter whether I've had a big meal. She hated the waiting with Viagra. Once, by the time I got hard, she had already decided to take a bath instead and locked me out! I went back to injections after that."

Serious side effects with injections are rare. Some men may be especially sensitive to the medicine and may end up with an erection that won't go away if they take too much of it. It is treated by injection of an opposite-acting medication, but it can be a major problem if the man is too embarrassed to go to the emergency room for treatment. Nevertheless, this should be a problem only at the very beginning when the doctor is trying to find the right dose, or if a man decides on his own to increase the dosage because he thinks he'll need extra for a date coming up. Scar tissue buildup within the penis can happen and can, though rarely, cause the penis to curve with erection. Finally, some men experience a burning discomfort within the penis from the medication, in which case they are unlikely to find the treatment acceptable to them. Alternative medications can be injected instead, however, to avoid the burning, but are generally available only from urologists who specialize in the treatment of erectile dysfunction.

Vacuum Devices

Vacuum devices are the Austin Powers–like gadgets that have been marketed as "penis pumps" in the past. Contrary to marketing claims, they don't increase penis size, but the medical-grade devices do allow impotent men to achieve a reasonable erection so they can have sex again. A band placed at the base of the penis traps the blood so that the penis stays firm.

Vacuum devices are mechanical, and many men find them awkward to use. But for some men, they are just the right choice. The main advantages are that they are completely noninvasive and work for almost any cause of impotence. One major complaint is that it can feel as if there is tourniquet at the base of the penis. This should not be too surprising, since there *is* a tourniquet at the base of the penis with this treatment.

Despite this, some men love the vacuum devices. One of my patients, Simon, is a successful businessman who retired at age fifty-five, only to have prostate cancer diagnosed two months later. He underwent radical prostate surgery, which left him completely impotent. Viagra was ineffective, and he didn't feel comfortable with penile injections.

"How's it going?" I asked when I saw him in follow-up, three months after he had been trained in the use of the vacuum device.

"My wife loves that vacuum pump!" he replied. "She says it's the best thing that ever happened to our sex life together. She says my penis is larger and fuller, and she gets great satisfaction from it."

"I'm glad your wife likes it," I said. "What about you?"

"Doctor," he replied very seriously with his hand clasped tightly on my shoulder, "I know you're a Harvard man and you have a room full of diplomas. But let me explain something to you about sex: if this vacuum pump makes my wife want to have sex with me, then I think it's fabulous!" And he chortled at his joke.

Penile Implants

There is an old urology joke about a woman who had adjustable breast implants placed so that she could avoid undue attention at work, but could increase their size when she so desired by flapping her arms, thus activating the pump placed in her armpits.

One day, sitting at a local bar after work, she meets an attractive man standing near her, and they hit it off. After a few drinks together, she begins to flap her arms to increase the prominence of her bust and says to the man invitingly, "Say, would you like to come over to my place for a nightcap?" To which the man replies "Sure!" and begins to pump his legs together, as a bulge developed in his pants.

Penile implants do not actually work by pumping the legs together, but the mechanism for the modern inflatable devices is indeed ingenious, and the devices have proved to be effective and reliable. Two hollow chambers are placed within the paired cavities of the penis, called the corpora cavernosa. A pump is placed inside the scrotum, as if it were a third testicle. When the man is ready to have sex, he squeezes the pump in the scrotum repeatedly, causing water to be transferred to the cylinders in the penis, thereby creating an erection. The implant mimics a true erection, since it puts fluid under pressure in the normal chambers of the penis. The difference is that the fluid is water instead of blood. When a man is finished, he deflates the implant by squeezing another area, the fluid goes back to its reservoir, and the penis becomes soft again.

The implants give a great result, cause no pain after the initial healing period, and allow sex to be completely spontaneous. Perhaps most important, these men psychologically feel as if they are cured. Dexter, a forty-three-year-old diabetic who had failed Viagra, put it this way: "Doctor, although injections worked for me and let me have sex again, I still felt impotent. But now that I have the implant, I don't feel impotent anymore. I don't know why. After all, I realize there's something artificial inside my body. It just feels different to me mentally, though."

One of the advantages of an implant is that the man can keep the penis erect for as long as he likes. This helps him maintain genital contact with his partner even after climax, which may help the woman achieve an orgasm, particularly if the man tends to ejaculate quickly.

The experience of being with a man with an implant may require a little adjustment in expectations for a woman. Hank, a fifty-three-year-old man, had implant surgery by me during the same operation as his radical prostatectomy for removal of a cancerous prostate by my colleague William DeWolf. Because of the location of his tumor, it was too dangerous to leave behind his nerves, and so the surgery meant that Hank would be impotent unless he had treatment. Hank chose an implant.

Although Hank had an excellent result from his implant surgery, he had difficulty with his partner, Alice. Alice was a pretty widow about six years his junior. They had met at the local golf club and had been dating for about six months when Hank was diagnosed with cancer. Their relationship had been very sexual until that point, and Hank was concerned about whether he would be able to maintain a sexual relationship after his operation.

When I saw Hank at his three-month follow-up visit, I asked him how things were going.

"Not too good, Doctor. Alice just isn't into me the way she was before. I don't know if we're going to make it."

"What's the problem?"

"She thinks there's something wrong with the implant. I do too. The sex just isn't the same."

When I examined Hank, the implant was perfect. It gave a natural appearance when flaccid and an excellent erection when inflated. It would have been difficult for someone who didn't know what was going on to tell that he'd had surgery for a penile prosthesis.

I told Hank that everything seemed fine, and he asked if he could bring in Alice to talk with me. Perhaps she could explain the problem better than he could.

Alice joined Hank in the office the next week. "Doctor, Hank's penis just isn't the same."

"Please tell me what you mean."

"Well, he's never hard around me unless he pumps it up." I explained that as a result of the cancer surgery, Hank's ability to have an erection on his own was gone. He was unable to get any new blood supply to the penis. This had been the reason to give Hank an implant in the first place.

"I guess I kind of understood it, but not completely," said Alice, looking disappointed. She had wanted me to be able to fix something that couldn't be fixed.

"You know, I wish I could give Hank back his own natural erections. But I can't. The implant is good, but it's not the same thing. However, it does let couples have sex in a way that's comfortable and usually satisfying." Alice didn't seem convinced. "Alice, I can see that something still disturbs you. Can you tell me what it is?"

Hank was sitting on the edge of his seat, as if he were hoping that Alice could identify the problem and I could correct it.

"This will probably sound awful, Doctor, but I may as well say it. When Hank and I started seeing each other, I really liked the way he was always hard around me. I would be at the kitchen sink washing something, and Hank would put his arms around me and I could tell he was excited by me. I could feel it in his pants." Hank smiled at this. It was obviously a pleasant memory for him too.

"But that doesn't happen anymore. Hank *tells* me that he's turned on by me, but how do I really know? I don't feel desired in the same way anymore."

"You're right, Alice. It *is* different now. I can easily understand why it doesn't seem as good to you. Before, you *knew*. Now you have to guess. But there are other ways to tell if a man is turned on by you."

"Really?" she asked. "How?"

"Just look at him, Alice, and see how he looks at you." From the way Hank looked at Alice the whole time they were together in my office, a blind man running for his life in the middle of the night would have known in an instant that Hank was crazy for her. "It's in his eyes, Alice. You're just going to have to trust it. Enjoy Hank, and let him enjoy you."

Alice smiled and said she would try.

Three months later, Hank had a big smile on his face and told me that he and Alice had just come back from the best vacation of their lives in the Bahamas and had more sex than he'd had in his entire life. "The implant's great, Doc. It's never let me down, if you'll excuse the joke. I think Alice is a believer in it now!"

The Perpetual Erection

Sometimes the ability to have a long-lasting erection artificially takes on a life of its own. After all, men fantasize about being able to have a strong erection that will last all day and night, and having an implant in theory makes this possible.

One of my patients, Edgar, is a bit of a hypochondriac and calls me whenever he notices something about his health that seems out of the ordinary. Edgar happens to have an inflatable penile prosthesis, and one day he called to let me know he was worried that there was something wrong with it.

"I think there's a valve problem, or the device has sprung a leak," he suggested. I was concerned when Edgar said this because both of those problems can occur with the prosthesis.

I had my fingers crossed during our conversation, hoping that Edgar did not need a new operation. "After how long does the penis start to lose rigidity?" I asked. I wasn't ready for the next answer.

"Well, it's been up now for six days, Doc," he said matter-of-factly.

"*Six days!*" I exclaimed, unsuccessfully trying to keep the astonishment out of my voice. I took a deep breath. "Are you unable to deflate it?"

"Oh, no, Doctor. I can deflate it anytime I want. The problem is that it won't *stay* hard."

"Edgar, these devices aren't designed to keep the penis firm that long. Why has it been up for six days?

"Oh, I keep it up most of the time, Doctor. I wear snug underwear and baggy pants, and so it doesn't really show. I just go about my business that way."

"But *why*, Edgar?"

"I like being hard. It makes me *feel better!*" he explained.

Clearly, men enjoy having a hard penis.

Alternatives in Action

Let's take a look at some case histories of how these alternatives to Viagra can work.

A Viagra Roller-Coaster Ride

Kurt was thirty-two years old when he came to see me, accompanied by his wife, Katrina. Their story illuminates some of the subtleties of human relations. Katrina was model-type gorgeous, wearing almost no makeup except for mascara and pale lipstick, with high cheekbones and shoulder-length auburn hair, and wearing stylish clothes. She would have stood out in any crowd. I was curious what their story might be.

"How can I help you?" I asked Kurt after we had all made our introductions.

"Doctor, we need some help in the sex department," answered Katrina with a trace of an accent before Kurt could form a response. "We've seen a lot of doctors in the past, but we were hoping that maybe you can help us." Kurt sat quietly in his chair watching Katrina, seeming a little annoyed that she was speaking for the two of them but not enough to say anything yet himself. "Kurt has an erection problem, and all the other doctors say it's in his head."

"Kurt, why don't you tell me your story," I suggested to him directly.

"Okay," he said, also with a slight accent. Kurt was slender, with an intellectual look, complete with scruffy, sparse beard. He and Katrina appeared somewhat out of place with each other: the revolutionary and the Fifth Avenue socialite.

"Katrina and I met in Texas, where I was getting an advanced degree in software engineering. Some mutual friends set us up, thinking we would hit it off because we were both Dutch. Sure enough, we liked each other a lot and started dating. But the first time we tried to have sex, I couldn't get it up. Not the next time either. Or the next."

"It seemed to go on like that forever," added Katrina, with a wry smile. "Finally, we saw a doctor together, and he prescribed Viagra."

"How did that work for you?" I asked Kurt.

"Great," he said, with only a hint of enthusiasm. "The first time I used it was the first time we ever had sex together. Then we started having sex all the time."

"Those were the good old times for us," added Katrina.

"After a short while, I found I didn't need the Viagra at all," continued Kurt. "I think I had just been intimidated by Katrina at the beginning, because she seemed so worldly. She knew everyone, and everyone knew her, and I kept wondering why she was hanging out with me. But once I got past the hurdle with Viagra, I was fine, and was happy to be able to give it up."

"Then why have you come to see me?"

"About a year later," explained Kurt, "after we had already been living together for a while, Katrina got a big job offer from a company in New York."

"It was the big break in business that I'd been looking for," jumped in Katrina. "I couldn't possibly turn it down, even though it meant trouble for Kurt and me. But Kurt was in graduate school, and neither of us planned to stay in Texas anyway. So I moved to Manhattan, and we spent all the money we didn't have flying back and forth and on crazy telephone bills.

"Kurt couldn't take it, though. He was convinced I was out on the town every night with a different guy. It didn't matter what I told him. He started going psychotic on me. When we did get together, Kurt started having trouble with erections again." Katrina looked at Kurt with tenderness.

"So, we got married. I hoped it would make Kurt relax and trust me. But it didn't help. We were still living apart while Kurt finished his degree, and he was stressed in every which way. Sometimes Viagra worked fine, sometimes not. Finally, Kurt graduated and got a job here in Boston with a biotechnology company on Route 128. I made a lateral move to a decent local company, and we were able to live together again."

"We had a great year and a half together. The sex was good again. And then suddenly it stopped."

"What happened?" I asked.

"His erections disappeared. It's been over a year now. We've seen a few different doctors, and all of them told us this had happened before, and it was all in Kurt's head. His physical examination is normal, and he's otherwise healthy. More than one of them said 'It's classic for psychogenic impotence.'"

"Kurt, what do you think?" I asked.

"I don't know, Doctor. It's true that it's been psychological in the past. That's obvious, the way that I had to use Viagra at the beginning and then I didn't need it anymore. But it feels a little different now. I don't wake up with erections. At least not hard ones. I've even tried to masturbate. My penis comes up, but it's really only semihard. Not like a real erection. Maybe that's all psychological too," he wondered aloud.

"Have you guys tried couples therapy or sexual counseling?"

Katrina nodded. "That was a complete waste of time," she said. "We did it quite a while ago, but it didn't work for us."

"What happened?"

"The doctor told us to be physical with each other without having sex. We were given directions about how I was supposed to touch Kurt's penis, without putting it inside."

"And . . . ," I prompted her.

"We did it a couple of times and then gave up. Kurt would lose the erection as soon as I tried to put him inside me."

"But I thought you understood that the point of the exercise was to not put the penis inside. The idea is for the man to gain confidence that he can achieve an erection and maintain it, and possibly that he can even regain it if he softens. No pressure."

"But that's crazy!" yelled Katrina. "What about me? I'm happy to do what I can to support Kurt, but I have my needs too! The whole idea was to get him hard. So once he was hard, I figured it was time for me to get mine. I was so frustrated. I felt like, 'If he's hard, let's do it.' Anyway, what's the point of talking about it? I'm not going to do counseling again."

Katrina had demonstrated one of the major challenges in dealing with sexual issues in a relationship: there are two people involved, each with individual needs and desires. A major goal of the behavioral therapy they had tried is for the man to gain confidence with sexual play that he can achieve an erection and can even regain an erection with his partner if he loses it for a while. The trick is to remove the anxiety related to inserting the penis in the vagina, and this is done by having the couple promise that they won't actually try to put the penis inside. Katrina short-circuited the potential benefits of the therapy because she wanted sex. Here's the erection, finally—let's go!

Although there were clearly aspects of Kurt's story that sounded psychogenic, I thought it would be helpful for Kurt to undergo studies to evaluate the blood vessels and nerves that control penile function. One of these involved measuring the arterial blood flow by ultrasound after creating an artificial erection with a penile injection. The results clearly showed a weak arterial flow. Kurt achieved a firm erection due to the strong nature of the medication, but he had an artery problem, most likely due to an injury of some sort in the area under the penis and scrotum called the perineum.

"Doctor, the injection was great," said Kurt when we met again. "It's been years since I was that hard. I definitely want to learn how to do that for myself."

"That's a fine solution for you, Kurt," I responded, and made arrangements for Kurt to be trained by my nurse, Kevin Flinn, a registered nurse, who has been working with me for ten years. "But I'm curious why this may have happened. Do you remember ever having an injury where you fell on something between your legs, like falling on the crossbar of a bicycle?"

Kurt thought for a moment. "No, I can't remember anything like that." After a moment, his face brightened as if he'd discovered something. "Wait a second! Just before I started having trouble again, I was water-skiing with Katrina during a vacation in western Massachusetts, and I had an accident. I ended up hitting my bottom hard on some rocks that were sticking up out of the water. It hurt bad for a few days, and I had a deep purple bruise for a while, but it all went away and I thought I was fine. Could that have been the problem?"

"Yes, it's definitely possible. I think your original problem was due to anxiety, Kurt, and Viagra then helped you. But the reason Viagra doesn't help anymore is that you now have a physical problem with your arteries that Viagra can't overcome."

Kurt looked relieved. "That's great news, Doctor!" he said, with more animation than I'd seen from him before.

"Why?" I asked.

"Because I knew this wasn't all in my head!" he said with obvious satisfaction, and looked to Katrina as if he had just proved an important point.

Katrina too looked relieved. "But if Viagra didn't work, Doctor, then why would injections work?" she asked. "You said the artery appeared damaged and couldn't carry the blood properly."

"Injections are a more powerful treatment than Viagra, Katrina, because the medication goes directly into the place it needs to work and can be given in very high concentrations. They don't always work either, but it's great that they seem to work well for Kurt."

A couple of months later, Kurt came back to see me in follow-up. He had shaved his beard and had cut his hair in a contemporary fashion instead of his graduate-student-long, messy free-form pattern. Kurt almost jumped out of his seat to pump my hand when I entered the room.

"How are you, Kurt?" I asked. I was surprised by his energy.

"Excellent, Doctor," he said with a broad smile. "The injections are fine. Sex is back to being the way it's supposed to be. Katrina and I are doing well again."

Kurt was still standing as I took my seat. Amazingly, I had barely noticed Katrina sitting there too because of the way that Kurt filled the room. I could imagine now for the first time Kurt's spirit when Katrina had met him, and it was easy to see why she had fallen for him.

"Please tell me what's been happening," I inquired.

Kurt was now able to have sex when he wanted and could last for an hour or more with the injections. He had his beautiful wife back at his side, appreciative of their lovemaking, and he no longer worried that she was going to leave him. This gave him room—permission, in a way—to go about and feel bold in his life once again.

"I'm a man again, Doctor," he said.

"A beautiful man," added Katrina.

"Thank you," they said together.

Overcoming a Long-Standing Medical Problem

Jim, an eighteen-year-old college freshman, came to see me, accompanied by his parents. At age five, he was found to have a tumor wrapped around critical structures in his pelvis. He underwent life-saving surgery that included removing the bladder and prostate, which meant that Jim needed to wear a bag over a little pink bud on his lower abdomen to collect the urine. In addition, the nerves that led to the penis were cut in order to remove the tumor.

Jim's parents were told at the time of the original surgery that Jim would never be able to have children of his own and would probably never be able to have sex. Now that Jim was an adult, he wanted to know for himself what the future held for him. Jim's father added that he knew that there had been many advances since the time of the original surgery, and they all wondered whether those advances might apply to Jim.

We spoke together about Jim's initial surgery and how he had done afterward. Remarkably, Jim had led an active and very normal life. He had played high school football as well other sports despite his urine bag hidden under his pads and uniform. He was a top student and had many interests and several good friends.

Jim's mother and father took turns talking, answering questions, but Jim had no problem adding his own point of view. He seemed well adjusted and comfortable with his mother and father, who were both lovely people. Eventually, I asked the parents to leave me alone with Jim so that we could discuss personal matters more freely, and they were happy to comply.

"So, Jim," I began, "what can you tell me about how your penis works? Does the penis ever get hard?"

"No," he replied. "I've seen movies, and read books and stuff, and so I know what's supposed to happen, but I've never had an erection."

"You've never woken up and noticed that the penis was hard or semihard?"

"Nope."

"I gather that since the urine doesn't come out of the penis, nothing else ever does either. Is that right?"

"Right."

"Have you ever had an orgasm?"

"I don't think so."

With the kind of surgery that Jim had undergone, everything that made the semen had been removed, so it can be tricky to figure out the orgasm business, since remarkably, some men can have the bells and whistles go off in their brain without any fluid coming out of the penis.

"Do you think about girls much?"

"Doctor, I do like girls. I've just never known what to do about them." Jim smiled, a little embarrassed by this disclosure.

"Have you ever had a girlfriend?" He shook his head to indicate he hadn't.

"Why not, Jim?" I asked.

"Well, a big part of it is that I feel any girl who saw me naked would be repulsed. I mean, who else carries their urine around with them in a bag on their belly? It's tough enough just to deal with other guys and their crazy comments. Girls would be even tougher for me.

"But the bigger part," he continued, "is that I'm just shy. I feel like a big dork around girls. But you know what, Doctor?" he added plaintively. "Even if I were really cool with girls, what could I ever do with them? How would I ever be able to have sex? My dad thinks you're going to give me Viagra to try, but even if it works, what am I supposed to do: take a pill the rest of my life every time I want to have sex? That doesn't sound too great."

"What other concerns do you have, Jim?"

Jim bit his lower lip and continued. "Apart from the girl thing, my life is actually pretty good. I'm in a good college, I'm doing well, I have friends, I play sports, and I know I'll have a solid job one day—something in finance, I think. My parents are really great. I see them, and I think I could be a great dad someday too. But if I can't have sex, and if no sperm comes out of my penis, does that mean that I can never be a father?"

The physical examination revealed Jim to be tall, lean, and muscular. He had what I call a swimmer's body: strong upper body, long lines, well proportioned. But Jim didn't swim much. He worried too much about his bag being visible. Instead, Jim's main sport now in college was basketball, and he told me he had a good jump shot.

In the lower abdomen, on the left side, Jim had a little pink bud of tissue peeking out from beneath a set of chiseled abdominal muscles. Over the bud sat a clear plastic pouch, like a Ziploc bag, with about an ounce of yellow urine. A special tape held the bag against the body, neat and trim. Jim was fastidious in the care he took of his body.

Jim's wanted his parents to come back into the room for our discussion.

"I have to say," I began, "how impressed I am with how you've all come through this as a family." Jim's mother smiled at her husband. I could see tears welling up in her eyes and handed her a box of tissues. Jim was beaming. Jim's father patted his wife on the back.

"Thank you," said Jim's father finally. "We've had a tough road to climb, but Jim's been a trouper all the way. You're right. He does have a great attitude. We weren't sure what the future held for any of us when Jim had his first surgery at age five, but it's turned out okay. Jim's turned out more than okay."

"But what can you do to help Jim?" asked his mother.

"What about Viagra?" asked his father, before I had a chance to respond to the first question.

"I think I have good news for you, overall," I replied. "Let's deal with the simpler issue first: fertility. When Jim had his surgery, his tubes were disconnected and rerouted. But the testicles feel healthy, and I have no doubt Jim is making healthy sperm. They just have nowhere to go. It's like a man who's had a vasectomy. Although we will likely never be able to hook up the tubes so that Jim ejaculates normally through his penis, I am almost certain that when Jim is ready to have children, we can collect sperm from the testicles, or the tubes around them, and use those sperm to make a baby with eggs from his partner."

Jim's family all exchanged glances. His mother spoke. "Doctor, we were told when Jim had his surgery that there was no possibility of Jim's ever fathering children."

"When Jim had his surgery thirteen years ago," I explained, "these techniques weren't available. There have been some wonderful advances since then in our ability to help men like Jim have children." Jim's mother sat back in her seat, clearly pleased with the new idea of being a grandmother one day.

"The erection issue is a little more complicated. The nerves that control erection were cut when Jim had his original surgery to remove the tumor. The penis itself is probably fine, but it never receives the signals that the brain is aroused, so it never gets hard. Men who have prostate cancer surgery often have the exact same problem."

"What about Viagra, Doctor?" asked Jim's father again.

"Unfortunately, Viagra doesn't work well in this situation," I replied. "Viagra makes the nerve signal stronger, but if there is no signal because the nerves are gone, then Viagra can't help." Jim's dad seemed disappointed.

"But there are a number of other treatments that work quite well," I continued, "and I am confident that we can find a way for Jim to have a good sex life whenever he's ready. The choices may not seem as simple as taking a pill, but they each have other features that are quite attractive."

"Like what?" Jim asked.

"The one that I would recommend for you now is to learn to inject medicine into the side of the penis that tells the blood vessels to create an erection, without depending on the nerves. The penis responds within a few minutes and can last a long time, even as long as a couple of hours in some men."

"Does it hurt?" Jim asked.

"It's a tiny needle," I explained. "Here, give me your hand," and Jim held it up for me as I had asked. I pinched the back of it slightly. "It's like that. You'll feel it, but it's not something to which you'll say 'Ouch.'"

"That's not so bad," he agreed. "But isn't there any other way to give the medicine besides a needle?"

"Yes, there is a tiny suppository that can be placed in the opening of the penis. But it's not as effective. In the long run, you might also want to consider surgery for a penile implant, but I would get you started now with injections."

"When do you suggest I learn how to do it, Doctor? Should I wait until I have a girlfriend? It seems kind of silly to get all needled up if there's no one to try it out with."

"Actually, Jim, I think you should learn to do it right away. Many men who have erection problems shy away from approaching women. If you knew you could have sex, it might give you the confidence to meet someone."

"Okay, Doc," Jim said with a kind of verbal swagger he hadn't exhibited before, "you've convinced me. Sign me up!"

Jim came back to see me three months later, this time without his parents. "How are you, Jim?" I asked.

"You won't believe what's happened to me, Doctor," he said with a broad grin. "I've got a girlfriend—Jenny. The injections work great. I stay hard for about an hour and a half. Jenny can't believe it. She says it's the best sex of her life. She really likes the fact that I stay hard so long."

"That's wonderful, Jim. How has Jenny reacted to your bag?"

"She's so cool about it, Doctor. The first time she saw it, she was all curious. I was embarrassed, but she said it was so clean looking—nothing like she'd imagined. Now it's no big deal at all."

"But the best part of the whole thing," Jim continued with excitement in his voice, "is that I have orgasms now! When you asked about it the first time I saw you, I really had no idea what you were talking about, even though I thought I did. What an incredible feeling! I can't get enough of it. Now I understand why people want sex so much!" he exclaimed, and we both had a laugh together.

"Yup," I responded, nodding my head to acknowledge the sentiment. "Welcome to the world of sexually active human beings, Jim!" and we laughed together again.

Learning from Viagra

As we have seen, impotence, or erectile dysfunction, can have profound effects on a man's sense of self-esteem and can even cause depression. It can also have major impact on relationships.

Viagra is an excellent treatment for many men, but there are many cases where it does not work. This is especially true for men with a physical cause for their erectile dysfunction. In general, the more severe the erectile dysfunction is, the less likely it is that Viagra will work. The important thing to remember, though, is that there are a variety of treatments that can work, even when

Viagra fails. None may seem as simple or elegant as taking a pill, but there may be definite advantages of these other treatments too.

Penile injections allowed Kurt to be his "old self," and he was able to restore the excitement of his relationship with Katrina.

Penile implants seem like a science-fiction story, or some version of the Bionic Man, yet they allow men to be spontaneous sexually without needing to take a pill, use a needle, or do anything else that seems unpleasant for them. Satisfaction rates are very high for them and their partners.

Vacuum devices have the advantage of being noninvasive. On the simplest level, they provide enough stiffness to the penis so that it can be inserted into the vagina. For many men and their partners, this is miracle enough.

Solving erection problems also often solves self-image problems and relationship problems. Even when there are clear psychological issues, it may be very difficult for one or both partners to accept psychological or sexual counseling as a treatment. Katrina never really bought into Kurt's behavioral therapy and ended up undermining it when his only problem was psychological, even when it appeared to be helping him. In other cases, it is the man who refuses to discuss relationship issues or even to attend a counseling session.

Making the erection better may be a good solution if the cause of the difficulties is the erection itself and other aspects of the relationship are reasonably solid. However, a firm erection cannot solve deeper problems.

Lessons

- Viagra is most effective for men with psychogenic impotence, working in approximately 80 percent of men. It is still effective in men with a physical cause of their erectile dysfunction but less so, working for roughly 65 percent of men with hypertension or vascular disease and in about 50 percent of men with more complicated medical conditions, which may include combinations of hypertension and diabetes.

- Other treatments are available that can be highly successful even when Viagra fails. It is important for men and women to be aware of this, so that they can have a reasonable expectation of success if they pursue treatment even after failing Viagra.

- Penile injections are most commonly used in Viagra failures. They are almost painless and create an erection within five to ten minutes. The erection may last a long time, up to several hours for some men (which can be an annoyance or a boon).

- Somewhat less effective is the same medication, alprostadil, in the form of a tiny suppository that is placed just within the opening of the penis. This avoids the use of a needle, which is useful for men with needle phobia.

- Vacuum devices create firmness in the penis by causing blood to run into the penis, where it is trapped by placing a band at the base.

- Penile implants, also called a penile prosthesis, are surgically placed within the penis. They can be simple, bendable rods or, more commonly, inflatable devices that create an erection as well as normal-appearing flaccid appearance. Many men feel that the implant makes them feel psychologically intact.

- Solving the impotence problem, with or without Viagra, can have an enormous impact on a man's sense of himself, his relationships, and the way that he interacts with the world.

Chapter Seven

The Viagra Myth in Gay Relationships

When Viagra first came out, I was curious as to what its impact would be in gay relationships. With heterosexual couples, only one partner has a penis, obviously, and Viagra is thus a treatment for half of the twosome. With gay couples, would both partners wind up taking the medication to enhance sexuality? Would a pill that improves the firmness of an erection be valued by those gay men who practice mainly oral sex, since in those cases the penis doesn't really have to "do anything"? Would a gay man with an erection problem be more or less likely than a straight man to hide his Viagra use from his partner? Does the Viagra Myth that a pill can solve personal and relationship issues play out differently if a man's sexual partner is male rather than female?

What has struck me as I have listened to the stories of my patients is that there are core issues that we all deal with, regardless of whether we are male or female, straight or gay. Nevertheless, gay sexuality does present some twists on heterosexual sexuality, and these show up with regard to Viagra.

How the Viagra Myth Is Different in Gay Relationships

The most obvious difference in gay relationships, of course, is that a man's partner is also a man and therefore also has a penis. As a result, expectation, desire, and awareness of one's partner's anatomy and sensitivities differ from heterosexual relationships. These differences can influence the reasons that a man may be interested in using Viagra.

Hard Enough for a Woman But Not for a Man

Jason was a thirty-two-year-old bisexual man who came to see me because he had noticed that his erections were no longer as firm as he thought they should be. "I can have sex, Doctor, and I don't have any problem with women, but I've started becoming a little self-conscious with men," he related. "I think I could really use a prescription for Viagra."

"Why are you only self-conscious with men?" I asked.

"I'm afraid that a man will know if there's something wrong with my erection."

"Why wouldn't you be afraid that a woman would be able to tell?"

"Women might play around with my penis, but in the end, the important thing for them is whether I'm firm enough to go inside. And I *can* go inside, even when I'm not that hard. But men know when I'm not hitting on all cylinders. They just know."

"Why do you say that?"

"Because every guy is a penis expert! They all have one themselves!"

Many gay men who have experimented with female partners before moving on to male partners say that one way that sex can be better is that other men know exactly what feels good for them. There is shared anatomy, after all, and, for almost all men, the shared experience of what it is to touch one's genitals and create pleasurable sensations. Being an owner of a penis does in fact appear to provide an advantage in providing sexual pleasure to another man. However, if a man is worried that his penis is not up to par, then there may be an added level of anxiety about having sex with another "penis expert."

Oddly enough, although it was only with women that Jason had a functional need for a firm erection in order to penetrate (since he did not practice anal intercourse), it was with his male partners that he was worried about diminished rigidity. He felt as if the microscope of sexual evaluation was focused on his penis when he was intimate with another man.

"If a guy sees that I'm not very hard, he might take it personally that he's not turning me on, or that I'm not that sexual, or there's something wrong with me. Any one of those might mean he won't be interested in seeing me again. I've been struggling with this for the last couple of years, and it's gotten to the point where I'm afraid to have sex."

"If this has been going on for so long, Jason, what brings you in to see me now? Is there something special going on?"

Jason sighed. "Actually, there is. I met someone. Douglas is really cool. And nice. We laugh a lot together. But the last few times we had sex together, I was fine until he started touching me. Once I begin having the thought that he'll know my penis isn't hard enough, I lose the erection altogether. The first time it happened, I was able to get the erection back, but not the last two times. Douglas said it was no big deal, but I felt like such an idiot. His penis is incredibly hard whenever we fool around, and I feel pathetic in comparison. I'm worried he'll drop me if I can't solve this problem."

"Jason, this is classic story of performance anxiety. I am confident your erections are quite normal in terms of blood flow and nerve function, but thinking about how you compare to him makes your mind get in the way of your penis. Viagra might help you get over the hump, so to speak, and once you become comfortable with your new friend, I suspect you won't need it anymore."

"Doctor, should I tell Douglas I'm taking Viagra?"

"If you really like him, I think it's best to be honest and open. Douglas realizes you've had a problem the last few times. If you explain that you're taking Viagra because you've been self-conscious and want to be able to have satisfying sex with him, I think he'll understand. Especially if he's as good a man as you say he is."

I gave Jason a prescription for Viagra and saw him a few weeks later. He was smiling from ear to ear when I stepped into the room. "Get this, Doctor: I took Viagra, and it worked great. I had a hard penis the whole time, and I didn't even worry about it when Douglas was touching me. Afterward, I decided to take your advice and told him I had taken Viagra. Guess what he said to me? He takes

Viagra too! Turns out he's always had a shy penis and uses the Viagra at the beginning of relationships until he's comfortable with his partner. We had a good laugh about how we were both trying so hard to impress each other on the outside but were so anxious on the inside."

"That's a great story, Jason."

"It gets even better, Doctor," he continued. "The next day, we both agreed to have sex without Viagra. I wasn't quite as hard, and neither was Douglas. But it was no big deal! I don't think I've ever felt as good about myself after sex as I did that time. I felt free."

The Danger of Poppers

A different problem with Viagra in the gay community is the occasional use of amyl nitrate, or "poppers," with sex. Poppers are sniffed to give men a feeling of euphoria that enhances the pleasurable sensations of sexual stimulation and orgasm. But they are also nitrates, and when nitrates are mixed with Viagra, they can cause a sudden and profound drop in blood pressure. Doctors are often aware of the use of poppers among gay men and caution gay men against mixing poppers with Viagra. But a man who obtains Viagra from his partner or on the street may have no idea that this can be a dangerous combination.

When Viagra came on the market in 1998, there was a rash of admissions to emergency rooms by men who had fainted or collapsed after taking the medication. Almost all of these men had taken Viagra even though they also took nitrates of one sort or another. No doctor would prescribe Viagra for men also taking nitrates, because this is the one known contraindication for Viagra. But these men coming into the emergency room hadn't received prescriptions for Viagra from their own doctors: they had received it from their lovers. Almost all of these men were gay.

Viagra is talked about so much and is in such frequent use that we forget that it is a prescription drug for a reason. Although Viagra is very safe overall, anyone who uses it must be aware of possible side effects. Not everyone can take Viagra under every condition. In particular, Viagra should never be taken with any type of nitrate medication or preparation, as this combination can cause serious trouble and must be avoided.

Sharing Prescriptions

The problem with sharing prescription medications is that there may be good medical reasons that a particular man should not be taking a specific treatment. Or there may be cautions that a doctor may give to his patient that may not be relayed to a partner. Or the dose of a medication may be different for different men.

Before Viagra was available, there was an even greater problem with men sharing prescription medications for erection problems. At that time, the most common treatment was penile injections. The worse the erection, the larger the dose of medication needed to create a firm erection. However, some men with normal blood vessels in the penis can have a superstrong response to even small amounts of the medication.

It was not uncommon, in the pre-Viagra days, for partners of gay patients to come into the emergency room with an erection that had lasted twelve hours or more. Although it sounds great to have an erection last so long, the penis often becomes quite sore after three hours or so, and as time goes on, it becomes really painful. This condition is called priapism. If the condition is untreated within the first four to six hours, the tissues inside the penis may become damaged, and the man can lose his ability to obtain erections.

In one of the worst cases I've seen, a man used his partner's medicine for an injection and then developed an erection that wouldn't go away. After two days, he finally came to the emergency room because of severe pain. The penis was massively swollen and discolored. "Why didn't you come in earlier?" I asked.

"It wasn't my medicine," he answered. "I knew it was stupid to do the injections, and I thought I would get in trouble for doing it. But I can't take it anymore." I was able to soften the penis, but his own erections never fully returned.

How the Viagra Myth Is Similar in Gay Relationships

In many ways, the core issues that arise with relationships and sexuality are similar whether one is gay or straight. However, there are a few wrinkles that are specific to gay men that come out with regard to Viagra and sexuality.

Performance or Permanence

Jimmy was a twenty-eight-year-old gay man who came to see me about having a circumcision. After discussing the pros and cons of the procedure, Jimmy asked, "Would you mind giving me a prescription for Viagra too?"

"Why, Jimmy? Are you having trouble with erections?"

"No, not at all. But Viagra is the bomb, Doctor. It turns me into a heat-seeking missile."

"I gather you've tried it before, then."

"Oh yeah, Doctor. Everyone I know uses Viagra whenever they get a chance. It's everywhere in the clubs. Some guys use it together with other drugs, like a cocktail, but not me."

"Well, if you can get it so easily, then why ask me for a prescription?"

"Cost. One hundred milligrams goes for twenty to thirty dollars a pop on the street, but it'll cost me only ten dollars each with a prescription."

"What does Viagra do for you, Jimmy? Why do call it 'the bomb'"?

"Viagra supercharges me. I don't really *need* Viagra, but it sure helps keep The Legend of Jimmy going strong."

Jimmy is not unusual in his wish to be "supercharged," and what he believed Viagra did for him socially and in terms of his self-concept as well. It is the Viagra Myth once again: the concept of using a pill to improve or even solve complicated personal and relationship issues.

Yet it should also be evident that Jimmy's use of Viagra is unlikely to land him in a committed relationship or even to begin a relationship based on integrity, honesty, or openness. Not that any of this is much on Jimmy's mind at this point in his life. Jimmy wants to be cool, get laid, and be seen as desirable.

In Jimmy's mind, Viagra helps him achieve these goals, and the way he describes his life and his use of Viagra is notably free of ambivalence. However, at some point, Jimmy may be looking for more in life and from his relationships. When he does, he will be faced with the same issues as any other man, gay or straight, who must balance the pressures of social and sexual performance with the desire to be loved for his authentic self.

What does it mean for a man's self-esteem if he believes he is attractive or sexually adequate only if he takes a little blue pill? What is the impact if he is fearful of allowing himself to be loved despite his inevitable imperfections? In a time when a medication that can enhance one's sexuality is so easily obtained, how does one balance the temptation to use it against the underlying desire, or perhaps fear, of simply being oneself?

"Jimmy, I'm afraid I can't give you a prescription for Viagra," I informed him.

"That's okay, Doctor. I just thought I would ask," he replied. Three months later, Jimmy returned to have his circumcision performed. He told me he was still using Viagra and still working on The Legend of Jimmy.

Lack of Desire

Jay was forty-one years old when he first came to see me. He was married, with a twelve-year-old daughter. "My family doctor told me to see you because I have no sexual desire, and I have osteoporosis," he explained, using the term for low bone density that can result in fractures from relatively minor trauma.

Jay was lean and trim, and his hair was cropped close to his head. It was springtime, and his sweater was perfectly wrapped over his back with the sleeves tied perfectly around his neck. His khakis boasted a crease that was done with great care by hand. Jay looked as if he would fit perfectly in Boston's South End, home to a thriving gay community. If he wasn't gay, I thought, he's doing a marvelous impression of someone who is.

As we spoke, it became clear that Jay had many of the symptoms of low testosterone, including diminished energy and slightly depressed mood. Osteoporosis is less common in men than in women, but it can be another sign of low testosterone.

"How are things going for you, sexually?" I inquired.

"My wife's great. We have a nice family, my daughter is doing well in school, and I love being home. I just have absolutely no desire to have sex with my wife, though."

"What about your internal hunger for sex?" I asked. "Any urge to masturbate, for instance?"

"Not really. Isn't that strange?" he asked me. "I feel completely asexual."

"Any outside partners or interest in someone outside the marriage?"

"No, Doctor," he said, taken aback. He smiled. "I'm a happily married man! To tell you the truth, it really doesn't bother me that I haven't had sex with my wife for over a year. She thinks it's strange, but it doesn't seem to bother her that much either."

Jay's blood tests confirmed low testosterone levels, and I started him on testosterone supplementation. Since low libido is a classic symptom of low testosterone, I was fairly confident that Jay would notice increased sex drive with treatment.

When Jay returned after three months, I asked him what he had noticed. "It's interesting, Doctor. My energy is definitely up, and I can lift more at the gym. I even wake up now and then with an erection, which I hadn't noticed in years. But there's no more desire than there was before."

Jay insisted he wasn't bothered in the slightest by the lack of desire, but he continued with testosterone treatments over the years with me, mainly to keep up the improvement in his bone density that had occurred in response to his testosterone treatment. Once a year, Jay would come see me for an examination and blood tests, and at each visit I would ask him if he wanted to do something to help him have sex with his wife.

"What do you have that might help me?" he asked. At first, I suggested penile injections or the vacuum device, but neither of those had any appeal at all for Jay. When intra-urethral suppositories became available, I offered those too. "No thanks, Doctor. My wife and I are fine. My daughter is doing well. There are more important things in a relationship than sex," he would say to me.

When Viagra became available a few years ago, we again had the same discussion. Jay was more interested than he had been in the past but again declined. "I'm just curious, because I've heard and read so much about Viagra," he told me. "But I still have no real sexual desire. My wife and I are doing fine, and my daughter is off to Dartmouth next fall. No need to rock the boat. Let's talk about it again next year."

The next year, Jay came in flushed and quite excited. "You'd better sit down for this," he warned me. "I have quite the news."

"What is it, Jay?" I asked as I took my chair while he remained standing.

"This is going to be a shocker for you," he prepared me. "I'm gay!" he blurted out.

"Wow!" I said, with genuine surprise. The surprise for me was not that Jay was gay but that he had finally discovered this about himself.

"I've been in therapy for years, and then, just a couple of weeks ago, it was like a light went on. It explains so much in my life!" Jay was thrilled with his discovery, and I was pleased for him.

"Have you talked to your wife about this?"

"Yes, and she's fine with it. She says she wasn't all that surprised. We've talked about it, and we're going to stay together. We have a great marriage, after all."

"What about sex?" I inquired.

"Oh that!" he pooh-poohed, as if I'd raised a trifling issue. "I'm still not interested. Even though I'm gay, I still intend to be faithful to my wedding vows and to my wife. I haven't had sex with a man, and I have no intentions of doing so. Gay is a state of mind and being, Doctor. It's not a requirement to have sex with other men," he explained to me.

Four months later, Jay appeared in the office, looking upset and agitated. "I need a prescription for Viagra," he blurted out as soon as he entered the room.

"What's going on, Jay?"

"I'm seeing someone. It's off and on, but my God, it's powerful. I think I'm in love. Or lust. I'm not sure which. But my brain is spinning, and I've got to do something."

"What do you mean, you've 'got to do something'?"

"His name is Maxwell. He's younger than me. A lot younger. And he's really built. I call him my Adonis. We were having sex the other day, and he dropped this comment about how my penis wasn't all that hard. We always tease each other about our difference in age, but when he said that thing about my penis and then laughed and called me an 'old man,' it bothered me. I thought I was doing pretty well, considering I hadn't had sex in so many years, and I was so new to everything.

"Afterward, he wouldn't return my calls like he did before. When we first got together, he would pick up on the first ring when I called him. Now, most of the time, he won't answer right away and I have to leave a message, and sometimes he won't call back until the next day. I think he's seeing someone else. Probably someone younger than me. I really need that Viagra!"

"Jay, take a deep breath and slow down. Let's back up for a moment. What's happening at home?"

"It's a mess. My wife told me to move out. She found me at home one day entertaining Maxwell, and she didn't like it. I had started going out a little bit, exploring my new self. I didn't see any reason why I couldn't bring someone home. We weren't doing anything, and it's my home too. But she didn't want it. She said it made her too uncomfortable. She said she didn't want to deny me whatever I needed to feel fulfilled, but that didn't mean she had to have her nose rubbed in it. So I left."

"How are you doing with that?"

"I've got myself a nice little place—very homey. Fireplace, exposed brick walls, bay window. I had a heart-to-heart talk with my daughter about it all. She didn't take it too well and won't talk to me right now. I know she'll come around eventually though."

"Jay, a lot has happened since I saw you just three months ago."

"Yes, it has. Not the least of it is that I've discovered how much I enjoy sex! I feel like an animal now. Except that apparently my Adonis doesn't agree with my estimation. He's such a child, really. He's only twenty-five. I don't know why I bother with him. But the idea of his being with some other guy while my phone call goes unanswered makes me see red!"

"Jay, have you been with other men?"

"Yes, yes," he said dismissively, as if it were a ridiculous question. It was hard to believe that only three months ago, he swore he had no need to have a physical relationship with a man, that it was enough for him simply to acknowledge intellectually that he was gay. "I've even broken a heart or two along the way," he said with apparent pride.

"And does your penis get hard?"

"Yes, it does. And not too bad for a forty-eight-year-old man, I might add. But forty-eight isn't the same as twenty-eight, is it? Are you going to give me the Viagra, or are you just building up to a lecture about how a man my age shouldn't be seeing a boy of twenty-five?"

"Jay, I'm just wondering whether there is something about the enormous upheavals and emotional stress of the last several months that is making you feel vulnerable, especially in your relationship with Maxwell. Who knows why he's not returning your calls as quickly as before, but I doubt it has to do with the firmness of your penis. I strongly doubt whether Viagra is part of the solution here."

"Doctor, I'm begging you. I don't know what else to do."

"Jay, are you still seeing your therapist?"

"No. I didn't see the need after he helped me figure out I was gay."

"Well, I'll make a deal with you. I think it's crucial that you have some support while you're going through this amazing but difficult time. I will give you a Viagra six-pack as long as you promise to call your therapist and arrange to see him again within the next few weeks. Deal?" I offered my hand.

"Deal," he replied and shook my hand.

Two weeks later, Jay came back. He started sobbing as soon as I entered the room. "He left me. Just like that. Told me he needed someone younger, with more energy. What a little . . ." and with that Jay suddenly pulled himself together, dried his eyes, and pulled back his shoulders.

"What happened?"

"We were on the ropes already when I saw you last time. I tried the Viagra. It didn't make a difference, and I felt like a druggie when I took it. My face got all warm, and my ears burned. I felt like anyone who looked at me could tell I was taking it. Might as well have made a sign saying 'Idiot on Viagra' and stuck it on my forehead.

"Taking Viagra made me angry at myself and angry at him. I can't believe I would do something like that just so a young kid would be impressed with me sexually."

"Jay, you don't need Viagra," I told him. Jay nodded his head in agreement. "And I'm sure you don't need Maxwell either." This time Jay looked up and scanned my face, listening closely. "The changes you've been through in the past several months are enough to lay any man low: recognizing that you're gay, dealing with the separation from your wife, coming to terms with your daughter, finding a new home, exploring a new lifestyle. You need a break! And some support. Did you ever make that appointment with your therapist?"

"I did. I have an appointment tomorrow."

"Good. Is there anyone else you can talk to?"

Jay smiled. "I've been talking to my mother. She's been incredible. I've told her everything, and it's all so simple for her. She says I'm her son, she loves me, and that's all there is to know." Jay seemed calmer. "I've had one conversation with my older brother too. He was always a tough guy growing up, and we didn't really get along. I told him, and he was okay with it. Turns out that everyone suspected all along that I was gay. Except me!"

We sat together for a moment in silence. Jay stood up, and I did too. "Thank you, Doctor. You've been a prince." I held out my hand, but Jay gave me a bear hug instead. He patted me on the back, said, "Thanks again," and left the office.

I didn't hear from Jay until a year later, when he returned for his annual visit. He was living with a man, this time only three years younger than him, in the same line of work. They had met at a weekend workshop, and Jay seemed quite happy.

"I can't believe all the drama I went through last year," he said. "My whole world turned upside down, and I thought I could solve everything in a flash by taking Viagra to make me younger. Life's good now."

"How are things with your daughter?"

"Great!" he replied. "She's a great kid. Young woman, I guess I should say. She's met my friend, Roger, and she's totally cool with it all. I'm doing okay with my wife too."

"What's happened to your sex drive?" I asked, recalling the years it had been absent.

"It's strong, Doctor," Jay said, smiling. "It makes me wonder whether it might have been strong even when my testosterone was low if only I hadn't been living a lie by trying to be straight."

"I wonder too, Jay. I'm glad it's all worked out for you. I was worried about you last year."

"I know you were, Doctor. Thanks for helping me see that I didn't need to base my happiness on a pill."

The Essence of Manhood

Anton was thirty-eight when he first came to see me about his erection problems. He owned a consulting firm and had been living with his partner, Benito, also thirty-eight, for five years. They were both HIV negative, and Anton was otherwise in good health.

"Doctor, my penis just doesn't get hard the way it should anymore. It's been going on this way for exactly five months. In fact, I could probably even pinpoint the day it changed for me. Do you think you can help me?"

"I hope so, Anton. Tell me, how does it affect you to have a softer penis?" I asked.

"Sexually, you mean?" and I nodded. "It's just not right. A man's supposed to be a certain way, feel a certain way."

"How has this made a difference in your lovemaking?"

"I think it's mental more than anything else, Doctor. There's something about having a really hard penis that feels good, all by itself. Wasn't it one of those famous gay Greek poets that said, 'A hard penis is the essence of a man'?

"I know it's a vicious circle, because the penis does get hard when I'm really aroused. But that hasn't happened in quite some time. I miss it and, to tell the truth, I'm worried there might be something wrong with me physically. And I'm less excited about having sex with Benito now, too. I tried Viagra a couple of times, but it didn't work right for me."

"What do you mean?"

"Well, it did make my penis harder, but I didn't like the feeling. It was artificial. I'm a warm-blooded, affectionate man. I shouldn't need to take a pill for that."

"Has Benito commented on things being different sexually?"

"No, but we don't have sex the same way anymore. He makes the occasional comment about how I've turned into wet firewood, or something like that."

"Wet firewood?" I asked, not understanding.

"Slow to get started," Anton explained, chuckling. "And sometimes it won't catch fire at all! But you know what? Just last week, I was the one who tried to get something started with Benito, and he never got hard. It's so odd. It's like we don't know how to be with each other anymore sexually."

"Anton, I'm curious about something you said earlier. You said that you could probably pinpoint the day everything changed for you, about five months ago. What happened then?"

"I remember it well, because I had just landed an important contract at work and was feeling great. All my life I've wanted to have a successful business, and here it was, actually happening, and Benito hit me hard that evening when I came home."

"What happened?"

"He told me he'd been thinking his life over and that he had decided that he wanted to have a marriage ceremony with me, and possibly consider adopting a child together. He wanted to do it as soon as possible. 'Life is passing me by, and I want to get this done,' he said. Ugh!"

"Why was that so unappealing to you?"

"Well there's a part of me that really does want to have a family. My dad was a great father, and I kind of assumed when I was a teenager that I would play out that role myself. Of course, being gay poses some challenges in that regard." His eyes rolled to the ceiling.

"So in a way I was thrilled that he asked me about it. It was the first time it ever came up in conversation. I do want to be married to Benito. I've got my own ideas about how to do it, though. I want it to be one humongous party. But it will take some planning. I can't do it on a moment's notice, like Benito wanted.

"Anyway, I felt really pressured when he asked me. I told him I couldn't do it now, and the worst part is that I wasn't very nice about the whole thing. I told him it wasn't fair for him to ask me to short-change my life dream to accommodate his emergency realization that he was getting older."

"How does this all fit in with the sexual troubles?"

"We tried to have sex that same night to ease the tension. Everything worked all right, but it was lousy sex, and I noticed that my penis wasn't all that firm. It's never been the same since that night."

"Have you talked to Benito about the ceremony issue again?"

"Not really. I think Benito's afraid to bring it up again, and I don't even begin to know what to say about it."

"What would you like to say about it?"

Anton inhaled deeply. "I'd tell Benito that I was sorry for being such a jerk about the conversation last time. What's the point of being successful if you can't share yourself with someone you love? And I would tell him that I want a commitment ceremony too, but with everyone I know attending. A really big bash: great food, a band, dancing. The whole nine yards."

"What about adopting a child?"

"If Benito really wanted it, I would do it too. It could be cool."

"Anton, you seem so much more animated than when you first came in. You talk about these things as if just the thought of them brings you pleasure."

"You're right, Doctor. It does feel good just to think about it."

"So why don't you talk to Benito?"

"When?"

"How about tonight?"

Anton gave a low whistle. "Wow. That's going to be a tough conversation. But I do need to clear the air." He seemed lost in thought for a moment. Then he looked straight at me again. "Thanks, Doctor. Of course, Benito and I have to talk, and I've been chickening out about it. I guess I needed a kick in the behind. But haven't you forgotten something?"

"What's that?" I asked.

"The reason I came to see you! What are you going to do to fix my erections?"

"Anton, I think your erection issue will fix itself if you can have an honest heart-to-heart talk with Benito."

"You really think so, Doctor?" he asked doubtfully.

"Just watch it happen," I reassured him.

A week later, I received a phone call from Anton. "Doctor, you were right! Benito and I had a talk the same night I saw you. I apologized, and he couldn't believe it. I don't think I'd ever apologized to him before. And as soon as we had our little catharsis, I felt the old sexual feelings come back."

"What are you going to do about the ceremony?"

"We've been working on it. It's been a lot of fun talking about it and planning it. It's going to be some party!" he said with obvious delight.

Learning from Viagra

The remarkable thing for me, as I have listened over the years to my gay patients describe their sexual problems and their experiences with Viagra, is how the core issues are so similar to those of straight men. There are some differences, of course, but mainly in the details. Having sex with another person, regardless of gender, is at once a primal urge and a conscious event that raises issues of whether one is attractive, lovable, appealing, and capable.

One similarity between gay and straight men is the pressure that men experience to perform well sexually. Indeed, especially when they are not yet in a committed, long-term relationship, men have a tendency to equate their attractiveness and self-confidence with their bedroom abilities. There is thus a powerful desire to use something that might enhance their erections, and Viagra has become a common choice for this.

The trap of the Viagra-enhanced erection is that it does not make the user more appealing as a human being or as a potential partner. Jimmy speaks as if he needs to maintain a certain image, the image of Super-Jimmy, and Viagra helps him achieve this in his own mind. I can't help but wonder what it would be like if Jimmy fell for someone who then discovered he had been secretly using Viagra all along. The inflated image Jimmy had created for himself would burst, leaving behind a disappointed lover and an embarrassed Jimmy.

Anton took Viagra in order to fix his lack of firm erections and diminished desire with his partner. But he was disappointed in Viagra because it didn't feel natural to him. Men with relationship issues frequently relate the same story when they take Viagra to solve their problem. "It just didn't feel right," they say, even though in many cases the penis did become firmer with Viagra.

Anton didn't need a blue pill to make his penis firm. Like Jay, he needed to sort out his personal and relationship issues. Anton didn't feel he was being honest with Benito or to himself. What Anton needed was to come clean with his feelings and desires. As soon as he did so with Benito, his normal passions and sexual energy were restored.

Nevertheless, there *are* differences for gay men. The fact that one's lover shares the same kind of sexual equipment creates opportunities for shared experiences and sexual discoveries, and there is a fairly automatic familiarity with what one's partner may be feeling. However, men feel sensitive about comparisons regarding penis size and firmness, and having a partner with the same anatomy can create a sense of awkwardness if one is less than confident about oneself. Viagra cannot change penis size, of course, but it may help with the performance anxiety that can compromise rigidity.

Viagra works very well to improve blood flow to the penis. But it is not a solution for concerns about one's sexual adequacy, and it does not replace the need for open communication in a relationship. There is no substitute in relationships, gay or straight, for honesty, openness, and integrity.

Lessons

- Many men, gay and straight, use Viagra in the hope that an improved erection will make them more sexually capable, and thus more attractive. For gay men in the intense and often promiscuous club scene, there may be a strong pressure to do whatever they can to enhance sexuality. Using Viagra may be a powerful temptation.

- As with straight men, the emotional cost of taking Viagra in this way is that it robs the gay man of being able to feel appealing and attractive just for himself. Furthermore, there is the risk of discovery and humiliation if a partner finds out that a man has been using Viagra secretly in order to impress the other person.

- Men who take Viagra when they don't really need it often feel as if they have compromised themselves in some core way. "Why did I have to do that?" they ask themselves.

- Having sex with another man adds an element of pressure, since one's partner is also a "penis owner" and therefore a "penis expert." Any degree of performance anxiety or self-consciousness regarding the appearance or rigidity of the penis is likely to be increased in a gay relationship because of this.

- Sharing of Viagra occurs commonly in gay relationships, since both partners are male. As a general rule, it is ill advised to share prescription medications, particularly because the actual patient may not be aware of circumstances that might create medical problems. With Viagra, the key point is never to combine it with nitrates of any kind, including amyl nitrate ("poppers"). Penile injection therapy can create serious problems if it is not performed under the careful guidance of a physician, and this treatment should never be shared under any circumstances.

- Viagra is a treatment to help blood flow to the penis. It is not a treatment for personal or relationship issues. Viagra is bound to be disappointing if a gay man takes it to rescue a failing relationship or because there are conflicts in the relationship that have created a loss of passion and a diminished sexual feeling.

- Both gay men and straight men tend to put too much emphasis on the value of a firm penis, particularly in relationships. Integrity, honesty, warmth, affection, thoughtfulness, and openness are qualities of an attractive, appealing partner and are much more important than whether a penis is "supercharged."

Chapter Eight

Viagra and Prostate Cancer

The most famous dictum in medicine is the Latin phrase *primum non nocere*, meaning, "first, do no harm." Yet despite this, physicians must take responsibility for causing large numbers of men in their fifties, sixties, and seventies to become impotent. They don't mean to do this, of course, but there it is. They do this in the name of curing cancer, specifically prostate cancer.

Prostate cancer is the most commonly diagnosed cancer in U.S. men and the second most common cause of cancer deaths, after lung cancer. The past ten to fifteen years have seen remarkable advances in prostate cancer screening and treatment, yet many men do their utmost to avoid seeing their doctor for prostate concerns because they fear that being diagnosed with cancer will mean the end of their life "as a man." Prostate cancer is so common in the United States that nearly every man older than fifty-five knows someone who has been treated. Although many men are still able to have their own natural erections afterward, many others will have trouble with erections.

The treatments for prostate cancer result in cure for a majority of men, particularly if the cancer was identified early. But once the men get over the shock of diagnosis and treatment, they come to see me for sexual problems. Some have already tried Viagra, and others want to know if it might be a solution for them.

How does the Viagra Myth play out for men who have been treated for prostate cancer? Is it true that a pill can undo the damage of surgery or radiation? What can a man do to regain his sexual life if he has come up on the short end of the Viagra Myth? And how does a woman deal with being supportive of her partner while still desiring a satisfying level of physical intimacy?

163

Advances in Treatment

Today, one of the most common operations performed in the United States is radical prostatectomy, the operation to remove the cancerous prostate. But back in 1984, when I started my training in urology at the Harvard Program in Urology based at the prestigious Brigham and Women's Hospital in Boston, there were almost no operations done for prostate cancer. Men who were diagnosed with prostate cancer received treatment with radiation therapy or no treatment at all.

The reason for this was that surgery was difficult, bloody, and associated with a high complication rate. Those complications included impotence in just about everyone, as well as an unacceptably high incidence of severe urinary leakage that required men to wear clamps on their penis so that they wouldn't drip.

Impotence resulted from damage during surgery to the nerves that control erection, since these run right next to the prostate, one on each side of it. At the time of my training, no one had a clear idea where the nerves were located or how they might be saved when the prostate was removed.

Unhappy patients make for unhappy surgeons, and because of the high complication rate, most urologists shied away from doing much prostate cancer surgery until a major advance appeared in the field.

Nerve-Sparing Surgery

The advance that made radical prostatectomy acceptable came in the early to mid-1980s, when a urologist at Johns Hopkins University named Patrick Walsh figured out a way to perform the surgery so that blood loss and urine leakage were minimized. But the most dramatic advance was that Dr. Walsh was able to identify the two nerves that control erection as they ran on both sides of the prostate and found a way to save them. (Incidentally, these nerves running next to the prostate are unrelated to the nerves that control sexual feeling in the penis or the ability to have an orgasm.

Those sensory nerves are not affected by surgery and never have been.)

He called this technique nerve-sparing radical prostatectomy, and remarkably, men were able to have erections again after surgery. As other urologists learned to do the operation, radical prostatectomy became a mainstay in the treatment of prostate cancer. Physicians and patients both liked the idea of the cancerous gland being entirely removed with the surgery, and surgery also added the benefit of being able to assess whether there had been any spread of cancer to the nearby lymph nodes. Surgeons embraced the operation once they could feel that they were not subjecting all their patients to certain impotence or a high risk of urinary misery. There are now roughly sixty thousand operations for prostate cancer done annually in the United States, most of them of the nerve-sparing type.

Unfortunately, expectations regarding the success of nerve-sparing surgery have been unduly high. Some centers report an 80 percent rate of return of erections, which brings in many men for surgery but creates a lot of disappointment. Studies in which the men themselves were asked whether they felt they had adequate erections for sex show that somewhere around half of men younger than sixty years old will have return of adequate erections, but this number drops to 20 to 30 percent for men older than sixty years.

Myth and Reality in Restoring Erectile Function

A common question I hear is, "If the surgeon saved my nerves, why don't I have my erections back?" Let me explain.

An erection occurs when the brain tells the blood vessels to fill the penis with blood. This signal is transmitted via the pelvic nerves, which run on both sides of the prostate. These two nerves are so close to the prostate that in order to save them, the surgeon must delicately dissect them off the side wall of the prostate. It can be difficult to identify the nerves in some cases, and it isn't always easy to spare them. If both nerves are cut or injured, it is impossible to have a spontaneous erection because the blood vessels in the penis don't even know they're supposed to be creating one. If one nerve is spared, erection is possible, but the success rate is only about 20 percent. If both nerves are spared, success is higher, but still no better than 50 percent in almost any surgeon's hands.

Why wouldn't a surgeon *always* try to save both nerves in order to give a man the best possible chance of getting his erections back? The reason is that there is a risk of leaving cancer behind by trying to skinny the nerves of the side of the prostate. A general rule in cancer surgery is to take as much extra normal-appearing tissue around the tumor or cancerous structure as possible, so that any microscopic spread into adjacent tissues can be removed at the same time, allowing cure in some of those cases. Since the erection nerves on both sides of the prostate are so close, sparing them means that no extra tissue can be removed, and there is a small but significant risk of leaving cancer cells behind too.

This is the dilemma for the surgeon and also for the informed patient who wishes to participate in his own decision making. Taking out the prostate with a wide margin of normal tissue increases the likelihood of complete removal of cancer on that side but reduces the chance of erections afterward, and provides no chance at all if a wide margin is taken on both sides. Sparing the nerves allows for the possibility of adequate erections afterward, but at the risk of leaving behind microscopic amounts of cancer on that side.

There is probably no other decision-making process in all of medicine that is quite like this one, which pits the hope of sexual function directly against doing the safest cancer operation. I do not want to suggest that men who undergo nerve-sparing operations are at great risk for cancer recurrence. But the issue is not a trifling one, and there are respected leaders in the field who oppose nerve-sparing entirely on the grounds that the operation has been misnamed and should more properly be called "cancer sparing" because of the avoidable risk of leaving cancer behind.

The decision to do unilateral nerve sparing (one-sided), bilateral nerve sparing (both sides), or no nerve sparing at all is influenced by several factors, including how extensive or aggressive the cancer seems to be. High-grade prostate cancers have a tendency to sneak out beyond the capsule of the gland, usually along the nerve pathways, and nerve sparing may be ill advised in those patients. Men with high levels of the cancer marker called PSA (prostate-specific antigen) are at increased risk of spread outside the prostate capsule too and may not be the best candidates for nerve sparing. Other men may have a nodule that makes the surgeon unwilling to spare the nerve on that side.

But why don't erections work in half or more of men even if the nerves were spared? In some cases, this is because the nerves were injured irreparably despite the surgeon's best attempts to save them. They are delicate structures, and there is no reliable way to tell if they are okay during surgery. It's entirely a wait-and-see evaluation: the ultimate return of erections is the only real test.

In other cases, the problem may not be with the two nerves at all but with the blood vessels that provide the increased flow and tumescence in the penis during satisfactory erections. These blood vessels sometimes don't function properly after surgery for prostate cancer, and no one really seems to understand yet why this may be the case. However, numerous studies performed on men who were normal before surgery but now have poor erections after bilateral nerve-sparing surgery do show that the ability of the penile arteries to fill the penis with blood can be impaired. Clearly, there is still much to learn about the response of the body to this type of surgery, and there remains considerable room for improvement.

"Yes, But Can You Stuff It In?"

There is an old joke that goes like this. The Jones family waits nervously to hear how the emergency surgery has gone for the elderly father of the household. Finally, after several anxious hours, the surgeon joins the family in the waiting area of the hospital. "The operation was a complete success," he reports with obvious satisfaction to the family. "Unfortunately, Mr. Jones died."

Something akin to this disconnect between the perceptions of surgeons and patients occurs in the area of nerve-sparing surgery.

The *Boston Globe* ran a recent article in which men from a prostate cancer support group expressed their resentment toward their surgeons because they felt they had been misinformed of the likelihood of having adequate postoperative erections. "Why do surgeons have to lie about their success rates?" complained one impotent cancer survivor who had undergone a nerve-sparing procedure. This is too harsh a criticism, but the discrepancy between what surgeons say and what patients experience is troubling. The explanation has a great deal to do with how one defines success.

The original definition for success with nerve-sparing was whether the penis was ever hard enough to penetrate, even if it happened only once. A prominent surgeon who took enormous pride in the results of his nerve-sparing surgery was overheard having a telephone conversation with a patient to determine whether the nerve sparing had worked. "Yes, but can you *stuff* it in?" the surgeon asked the patient. If the answer had been yes, this would have counted as a success. However, no man with a "stuffable" erection is going to strut around feeling like a great lover. Yet if the penis fills up with blood with stimulation or arousal, then at least one nerve must be intact, and the surgeon can declare a success.

The first reports on the return of erections after nerve sparing were all presented by the surgeons themselves, interpreting what their patients told them in the office. These rates of success were all very high. But when someone other than the surgeon talked to the patients and defined success by whether the patient considered himself to have adequate erections, the reports were much less impressive.

The Waiting Game

One of the more difficult aspects of the nerve-sparing surgery is that even if the erections do return, it may take up to a year or more for this to happen. In the meantime, the penis is always flaccid, and a man must wait to see whether he is in the lucky group. The reason is that the nerves can take that long to recover from surgery, or in some cases to actually regenerate after injury. "I wake up every morning and check under the blankets for any signs of life," reported Andy, who had undergone nerve-sparing surgery six months earlier.

A substantial proportion of men who do have return of erections begin to notice "signs of life" only after nine to twelve months, so a completely "dead" penis for the first several months doesn't mean much. But the waiting game does take its toll. A study published several years ago showed that many men demonstrate symptoms of depression that show up only twelve months after surgery for prostate cancer. I am certain that the explanation is that men hold onto hope for twelve months that their own erections will return, but then become shattered by the realization that they are now stuck with an unresponsive penis. Men hear they must wait one year to learn whether their erections will return. When the anniversary of their surgery passes they give up hope, and come to grips with the realization that they are impotent.

Does Viagra Work?

Even if a man and his surgeon are both hopeful that erections will eventually return, there is no reason that the man can't get some help while he's waiting. Viagra is the obvious solution. "Just give me some of those Viagra six packs," urged Randall when he saw me two months after his surgery. "They worked before surgery, so I'm sure they'll work for me now." Unfortunately, it's not so simple or all that effective.

Viagra works by enhancing the nerve signal in the penis to create an erection. If both nerves have been injured and there is no signal, Viagra has no opportunity to enhance the signal. Viagra simply does not work if neither nerve has been spared during radical prostatectomy.

Even if the nerves *have* been spared, the results are less than glorious. Viagra salvages adequate erections in about 40 to 50 percent of impotent men if both nerves have been spared and in only about 25 percent if one nerve has been spared. It is true, though, that it takes a while for the nerves to regrow, or heal. Since Viagra needs those nerves to be putting out a signal, men who failed a trial of Viagra soon after surgery should definitely try it again several months later, when they may have a much better response. In my experience, though, Viagra has no chance of working unless the man has already started to notice some "life" under the blankets, even if it is only a fullness of the penis that occurs.

Radiation and Seeds

As disappointment with surgery became more publicized, men turned back to the earlier treatment for prostate cancer: radiation therapy. The standard form of radiation therapy is called external beam therapy and consists of approximately two months of daily treatments, more or less like a prolonged x-ray focused on the prostate and surrounding areas in the pelvis. It is painless but can cause irritation to the bowels and bladder; men may find that they have frequent bowel movements and urination and may develop bleeding from both sources.

In contrast to surgery, which causes men to be impotent immediately, even if the erections eventually return, radiation does not usually affect erections for quite some time. Because sex does not appear to be affected by radiation right away, men often have the impression that radiation treatment is better for a man who desires to maintain his sexual functioning.

Unfortunately, radiation is also trouble for erections. It's just that the bad effects may be delayed for twelve to twenty-four months. When the erections do begin to weaken, the process tends to be gradual, and because it is separated in time from the radiation treatment, many affected men don't even recognize that the radiation may have been the culprit. However, studies show clearly that after two years, erection rates are similar for both radiation and surgery.

A newer form of radiation treatment has appeared, called brachytherapy, or seed therapy. In this treatment, tiny pellets (the "seeds") are placed throughout the prostate while the man is asleep under general anesthesia. The radioactivity acts in a small surrounding area, with the entire prostate being treated by having appropriate placement of the multiple seeds. After a couple of months, the radioactivity has dissipated.

Men like brachytherapy because it is a one-time event, and they can then go on with their lives. There is also a theoretical advantage in terms of side effects, since the radiation should be localized only to the prostate, sparing the nearby penis. Yet this does not seem to be true so far. Clearly, some men do maintain their erections after brachytherapy, but I also see many men who have erection problems that developed after seed therapy.

Viagra does work for many men who experience erection problems after radiation therapy or seed therapy, particularly if the problem is simply a degree of diminished firmness. But to my mind, the most important thing that men and their partners should know is that even if Viagra doesn't work, there is always a way for men to be able to resume satisfying sexual relations. The treatment of sexual problems for men with prostate cancer does not begin and end with Viagra. Let's see how this all plays out emotionally for men and their partners.

"I Can't Wait Forever for These Nerves to Grow Back!"

Earvin was a sixty-three-year-old married man who came to see me eight months after a radical prostatectomy. He was referred by a colleague who does prostate cancer surgery but is not interested in treating erection problems that arise from it. (There's nothing wrong with that, by the way. By referring patients to an appropriate source, he is, in a way, addressing the problem. Sexual issues just aren't his cup of tea. But radical prostatectomy is, and he does an excellent job with it.)

"Doctor, I really need your help here," said Earvin, as his wife, Jacquie, sat quietly next to him. "I'm grateful to my other doctor for finding my cancer early, and so far it looks like I'm cured. But without my erections, I feel like an old man. My surgeon told me that the erection might not come back until a year or more has passed from my original operation. But it's been eight months now. I can't wait forever for the nerves to grow back! I've got a beautiful young wife, and I need to be able to take care of her." Jacquie protested gently, her eyes twinkling.

"Doctor, I've got a friend who had prostate surgery. He swears by Viagra. He says it's the fountain of youth, especially after his prostate cancer. So I pestered my other doctor until he gave me a prescription, but it didn't do a darn thing. What's the story with that? I thought Viagra always worked! Now I'm a wreck. I'm afraid that if Viagra doesn't work, there's no hope that my own erections will ever come back either. Is there any hope for me? I'm not ready to be put out to pasture."

Finding the Best Treatment

Earvin had done all the right things when he had taken Viagra. It just wasn't the solution for him at this time.

"Earvin," I said, "your doctor was right in telling you that your own erections may come back in a few months. But there's no reason for you to wait. You should be having sex as soon as possible!"

"Doctor, I knew I liked you as soon as you stepped in the room!" he exclaimed, and looked toward Jacquie with satisfaction. I had Earvin learn to do injections, and by the end of his third visit he was on his way to spiritual recovery.

Earvin and Jacquie returned after another three months. Amazingly, Earvin *did* look younger. "Hey, Doc. That's some fantastic arrow poison you've got there. My lady and I are grateful to you for providing us with a version of the fountain of youth. We go at it like we used to. To tell the truth, these erections now are even better than what I was able to do on my own before surgery. Who knew that was possible?" he roared with bravado. "Every once in a while, I feel like my own erections might just be good enough too. I wonder if the injections jump-started something down there."

I told Earvin about the Italian study of men having better return of their own erections after doing penile injections. "But more likely, Earvin, the nerves in your penis are starting to heal and make the proper connections again. It's entirely possible that soon you might be able to give up the injections altogether or that Viagra might work for you now."

Earvin's eyes opened wide. For some men, Viagra has this aura of creating supermen, and Earvin seemed intrigued. "Doctor, I've run out of my old Viagra, but I'd really like to try it again if you think there's a chance it might work. Would you give me prescription?"

"Sure, Earvin, I'd be happy to have you try it."

"Make sure it's the strongest dose possible," he said, winking at me. Earvin dropped his substantial left hand on Jacquie's right knee and shook it, as if bucking her up for a new adventure together.

Several months later, Earvin returned for a routine visit with me. As always, Jacquie was by his side.

"I can get a semifirm erection on my own now, Doctor, but it's not great. I still use the injections most of the time, but every once in a while, I can just get by on my own, without anything. I give credit to my lady here, because if she weren't so beautiful, I *know* it would have been impossible for me." Jacquie blushed at the compliment, as she seemed to do whenever Earvin talked this way.

"What about the Viagra?" I asked.

"Oh, we gave that up," replied Earvin. "It did help, but Jacquie and I need sex to be *spontaneous*!" he said, emphasizing the last word as if it were the key to life.

"But Earvin, how can sex be spontaneous if you use injections?" I asked.

"Doctor, the needle takes me only a moment. Jacquie likes to take a moment in the washroom before we get all hot and heavy anyway, and by the time she comes out, I'm ready for her. With Viagra, we had to pay attention to meals and timing, and it just wasn't for us." I'd heard this before from other patients, but I found it fascinating that a man would experience an injection into his penis as spontaneous.

"Don't be sad about the Viagra, Doctor," he continued, as if he had sensed some disappointment on my part. "Jacquie still feels I'm a tiger without it, and I feel like a young man again. You did good by me, Doctor. You really did."

Alvin and His Second Chance

Alvin was forty-six when he first came to see me. He was a high-powered executive from a financial services company, trying to make his way to the top. At a recent meeting of the CEO and his lieutenants, the CEO described how his prostate cancer had been detected by the blood test PSA and how it had saved his life because the cancer had been detected so early. The CEO suggested that all the men in the room have their PSA checked too.

Although Alvin was under fifty, the recommended age for beginning prostate cancer screening, he went ahead and asked his doctor to do the test during his routine physical. Sure enough, his PSA was abnormally elevated, and a biopsy revealed cancer. Moreover, the cancer was an aggressive type.

The urologist Alvin consulted recommended that he undergo surgery to remove the prostate, and because the cancer appeared so aggressive, he further recommended that no attempt be made to save the nerves: trying to save the nerves ran a risk of leaving nearby cancer cells in the body. Alvin was referred to me to address the sexual issues that were certain to occur as a result of his surgery.

Isolation and Despair

Alvin had come alone to his visit. He was divorced, with two teenage children. He was dressed impeccably in an expensive-looking navy pinstripe suit and wingtip shoes. He was talking on his cell phone as I walked in, but he immediately said, "Gotta go," snapped shut his phone, and put it away.

"Doctor, I can't believe this is happening to me. The last three weeks have been a blur. One day I'm fine, and the next I've got cancer. Then right after that, I learn that if I want to live, I'm going to have to give up my sex life forever. Or at least the way I've known it. The other doctor told me to see you before surgery to 'become educated' is how he put it, about what the future might hold for me in terms of sex."

Alvin was pleasant to talk with, and it was easy to identify with his situation and to feel his distress. He loved his children and basically spent almost all of his week either with the children or working long hours. He had a girlfriend who was thirty-two, from Brazil, and they saw each other only about once a week or less.

"My sex life now is the best it's ever been in my life, Doctor. Man, I wish I knew this stuff when I was eighteen years old," he mused. "This girl I've been seeing, Claudia, she's a hot ticket. She's full of life. She's always ready to have sex with me. It's fantastic. I don't feel forty-six with her. She makes me feel alive. What am I going to do now?" he asked. "Thank goodness there's Viagra for me, right?"

"Alvin, it's important that you know that this operation in no way means that this will be the end of your sex life. But it's unlikely that Viagra will be the answer for you."

"What are you talking about, Doctor? Everyone knows Viagra is the real deal. I've even tried it already a couple of times with Claudia. Gave me a nice feeling in the penis. If it worked once, it should work again, right?"

"The problem, Alvin, is that after this operation, the nerves that control erection will be cut, and Viagra needs those nerves to be okay in order for it to work."

"What are you saying?" Alvin asked, aghast. "Are you saying Viagra's not going to work for me? What am I going to do then?" he asked with increasing agitation.

"Alvin, I'm sure that you'll be able to have sex again in a way that will be satisfying for you. It's just that it's unlikely that Viagra, or any other pill, is going to be the way to go."

Alvin sat down, looked down at the floor, then back up at me. "When I left my wife a few years ago, it wasn't a rash decision, even though no one seemed to understand it. I needed to start over with my life. I was unhappy. I'm glad I did it, but it's been a tough road. Lonely. I don't see my kids enough, but even more, it's female companionship that I miss.

"I never felt like an attractive person when I was married. My ex-wife criticized me for everything—the clothes I wore, the way I spoke. Although we had a lot of sex when we first met, it stopped almost completely the day we married. It's just like the jokes guys tell, but it was true for me and not very funny.

"But as I started getting my life back together, I started meeting women too. Then I met Claudia. She's passionate and fun, completely different from my ex-wife. It made me feel great that she would want to be with me. The funny thing is that she thinks I'm a great lover! I love that feeling. Now, here I am, forty-six years old, single, alone, except for this hot mama I'm seeing, and I've got this decision to either get my cancer removed or keep my sex life going a little while longer! It's not fair. I'm not ready to die, and I'm not ready to be an old man."

Suddenly, Alvin's body shook, as if he'd had a minor convulsion. "I'm scared," he whispered, and looked up at me, searching my eyes.

"What are you scared of, Alvin?"

"I'm scared of dying. I'm scared Claudia won't want anything to do with me if I can't have a normal erection. I'm scared that if she leaves me, there's no way I can ever find another normal woman, let alone a sexy one like Claudia."

The Talking Cure

"Alvin, you've got a lot to deal with right now. Here's how I can help you. On a medical level, you should understand that you will definitely be able to have sex again, although it won't be exactly the same as it is now. But on an emotional level, it's clear to me that you need some support. Is there anyone you can talk to? Claudia, maybe?"

"Not really. I've got friends, but I wouldn't be comfortable talking to them about this stuff. As for Claudia, all we ever talk about is plans for the weekend or movies. Nothing personal. I guess I keep her at arm's length. I'm afraid it would turn her off if I spoke to her about emotional things. She would see me as weak."

"You might be pleasantly surprised how Claudia responds."

I explained about penile injections, implants, and vacuum devices. "There's something else you might want to consider, Alvin. In men who are going to have prostate cancer surgery where the nerves will not be saved, as in your case, we offer the chance to have a penile prosthesis placed during the same operation. It consists of two hollow cylinders that are placed inside the two natural chambers of the penis that normally fill up with blood to give you an erection. A small pump goes inside the scrotum, as if you had a third testicle. When you want to have sex, you find the pump in your scrotum, give it a few squeezes, and the penis stands up. When you're done, you squeeze a different area and the penis goes down. Once you heal up, the penis looks normal and feels normal, and sex is easy. We call placement of the prosthesis with the prostate operation 'immediate sexual rehabilitation.' Most men are able to have sex again soon afterward, often by six weeks."

"Isn't it dangerous to do two operations at once?"

"No. All we've done is borrow a page from the women's experience with mastectomy. Some of those women do great by having their breast reconstructed at the same time that it was removed. My colleague and I have been doing this for ten years now in over 150 men, and it's worked out very well for them."

"But what's it like to have an implant in my penis? Doesn't it look weird?"

"The great thing about an implant is that the penis looks normal and feels normal, and sex is easy and spontaneous. If you've ever taken a shower at a health club, you've probably seen men with implants, and you didn't know it. They look very natural, both when they're up and when they're down."

"What do you think Claudia would say about it?"

"Why don't you ask her? Bring Claudia to your next appointment, and we can show both of you what it's all about." Alvin agreed.

Alvin returned with Claudia a week later. She was indeed a beautiful young woman, and she seemed very taken with Alvin. Claudia held Alvin's arm as they sat next to each other in the consultation room.

"Alvin's told me about the things you can offer him sexually," Claudia began. "He thought it would be a good idea if I came in today. I hope that's okay with you."

"Of course," I replied. "In fact, men do much better when their partners become involved in their treatment. They feel less burdened by their decisions. Besides, women tend to ask better questions than men about treatments," I said, and Claudia smiled.

I went on: "The specific thing I wanted Alvin to think about prior to surgery is whether he was interested in having a penile prosthesis placed at the same time as his prostate surgery. It's the best time to do it, since everything is done at once and he can recover from both operations at the same time. If it's not right for you now, Alvin, we can go ahead with all other treatments later, but I wanted you to have the opportunity to consider it now. It's like with a car: if the hood is open, you might as well take care of all the engine problems at once."

"How do couples deal with the implant during sex?" Claudia asked. "I mean, do men pump it up before even beginning foreplay, or do they have to stop everything in the middle to get it up?"

"One of the nice things about the implant," I explained, "is it allows couples to have spontaneous sex. It usually takes less than thirty seconds for the penis to become completely hard. So even if a couple needs to stop what they're doing to make it hard, it's not much of a delay. Some men pump it up at the beginning, and others wait until later."

"Doctor, what is it like for a woman if her partner has an implant?"

"It depends a lot on the woman," I answered. "The penis itself looks very much the same, and the erection itself is very firm. The penis even stays firm after the man has a climax, so some men feel as if they are a big stud with it." Claudia and Alvin smiled at each other.

"So it feels the same for a woman once it's inside?"

"Yes."

"What do women say they *don't* like about the implant, Doctor?"

"Satisfaction rates for women are extremely high, Claudia. I think the biggest problem for some women is that they miss knowing exactly when their man is excited, because the implant makes the penis firm only when it is pumped up."

"Will it be dangerous for Alvin?"

"There are two main risks. One is infection, which occurs in 1 to 2 percent of men and requires that the device be removed. And the other is that the device will eventually fail. This can happen anytime, even as soon as one year later, although on average they last ten to fifteen years. If it fails, another operation is required to replace it."

"Alvin, honey, it sounds like this is a great solution for you," she said enthusiastically, and with a warm smile. "It sounds as if we could still have a lot of fun with the implant. I didn't like the other choices you mentioned."

"But it's not Viagra," Alvin complained to her.

"Viagra's not one of our choices, though, so who cares about Viagra?" Claudia argued back.

Alvin turned to me. "We've been talking, Doctor, as you can see. Claudia's been great. I didn't know how great she could be until I gave her a chance to be."

A couple of weeks later, Alvin had his combined surgery for the prostate and the penile implant. Everything went well. Claudia was waiting for him afterward, together with Alvin's brother, who had flown in from Chicago. I learned later that the week before surgery was the first that Claudia and Alvin's brother had learned of the other's existence. It seemed that Alvin had kept his personal life at arm's length from everyone.

Three months later, Alvin returned to the office with Claudia. He looked fit and tan. The creases were gone from his forehead. "How's it going?" I asked.

"I can't say it's exactly the same as it was before the surgery, Doctor, but there's no question that both Claudia and I are pleased. We have sex whenever we want, and I don't really think about the implant anymore. I even take showers at the gym now, and like you said, no one even notices. But there's something else, Doctor, that I need to mention."

"What's that, Alvin?"

"This whole cancer thing changed my life completely. For the better. I know it sounds weird, and I wish I didn't have cancer, but I feel more alive now, and thanks in no small part to you, my life is actually fuller." He paused for a moment to reflect. "Claudia turns out to be a fabulous partner for me." He glanced at her, and I could feel the warmth between them. "She's been incredible. I can talk to her, and it makes such a difference. So I've asked Claudia to marry me, and she's accepted."

"Congratulations to both of you! That's wonderful news."

"But there's more, Doctor. I have a relationship with my brother now too. In fact, I've discovered all these people around me who have been great, but I just never let them into my personal space. You encouraged me to trust Claudia by sharing my fears, and it started a positive cycle that's changed my life. So, thank you, Doctor. It's been quite some journey these past months."

What Is a Woman to Do?

It's hard for women to know how to deal with their partners as they anticipate prostate cancer treatment. Of course, they want to encourage their partners to do what is best for them, and survival from cancer is usually the most important consideration.

But what about sexual satisfaction? Is it all right for a woman to acknowledge that she would like to be able to have sex after her partner's treatment? Or does this perhaps put undue pressure on the man to have a lesser treatment in order to be able to satisfy her request or need? Or is it best for a woman to be self-denying, and to say, "No, no, it's okay. I don't want or need sex anymore anyway"? And what about if a woman doesn't really care for sex in the first place?

A Disapproving Partner

One time I was counseling a couple about sexual options prior to the man's upcoming surgery for prostate cancer. When I came around finally to talking about the advantages of implants compared to other treatments, the man's head was nodding along as I spoke, as if to say, "Yes, yes, yes." Comically, his wife next to him was shaking her head back and forth at the very same time, as if to say, "No, no, no."

When I finished my piece, I asked them both if they had any questions. "No, you've been very thorough," said the husband. "Honey," he said, turning to his wife, "what do you think of the implant?"

"It's not for you," she responded.

"Oh," said her husband, obviously crestfallen.

"Why do say that?" I inquired.

"Doctor, there's no way that I would ever want my husband to have something artificial inside him like that. It's not natural. Who knows what might happen with something like that."

"But men and women have artificial devices placed inside their bodies every day," I countered. "Heart valves, artificial blood vessels, pacemakers, new knees and hips. These artificial devices aren't new or mysterious, and they allow people to lead more comfortable and pleasurable lives."

"That may be, Doctor, but an implant in the penis? It's not for him."

This time her husband piped up. "But why, honey? We could have sex again, just like we did in the good old days."

"What I care about now," she answered firmly, "is that you're healthy and that you'll be able to keep me company for another sixty years. Besides, I hadn't gone through menopause in the 'good old days.' Why would I want you chasing me again like that? We're not so young anymore. Let's leave well enough alone, and if we want, we can look into these things again after your surgery."

Not surprisingly, they never came back to see me. For some women who have reached a certain age, sex is simply not such a priority. Perhaps it never was for them. But companionship is a different story, and so is the health of one's partner. If sex is not a priority, why on earth would one take even the slightest risk for it?

An Open Mind

Jill and Harold were a different kind of couple altogether. Harold was a fifty-six-year-old school teacher from a small town in New Hampshire who had researched his options on the Internet after being diagnosed locally with prostate cancer. Harold and Jill had decided to drive three hours to take advantage of Boston's well-deserved reputation as one of the top places in the world to receive medical care. After consulting with doctors at the Dana Farber Cancer Institute, they were referred to me to learn more about what they might expect after Harold's cancer treatment and what they might also be able to do to restore their sex life if Harold developed impotence.

Jill was the town librarian and was a year younger than Harold. They had married young and had two grown children who were on their own now.

"This sex thing is pretty important to both of us," Jill informed me. "Well, maybe I should say it's pretty important to *me*," she said in a loud voice, and both of them laughed together. "As a matter of fact," she continued, "if there is really any risk of Harold's being unable to have an erection after treatment, perhaps you could provide us with a bucket full of Viagra so we can get our licks in while we can!" And they both laughed heartily again.

When I asked what they had decided to do for treatment of the cancer, Harold replied, "I'm going for the nerve-sparing surgery. No question about it."

"The more nerves, the better!" interjected Jill.

"Seriously, Doctor," continued Harold, "what's the point of being alive if you can't enjoy yourself?"

"We understand that nerve sparing might not work," said Jill. "In that case, we'll just go on to Plan B, and you can prescribe Viagra, or injections, or whatever else you think will work. But we're going to give the surgery a chance, and then we'll see what we need to do. We're having too much fun with sex to just give it up without a fight! Right, honey?" she cooed, puckering up in a theatrical pose for a kiss. Harold pinched her side, and Jill gave a little yelp in mock pain.

"Jill and I have been pretty lucky, Doctor," said Harold in a more serious voice. "We know nothing is guaranteed in life and that it all can be taken away from you in an instant. That's why we try to squeeze as much out of every moment as we can."

Harold and Jill had a wonderful attitude about life and an open way of dealing with sex. Harold did well with his surgery and appeared to have been cured of his cancer. But for six months after surgery, he feared that his penis would never stand up on its own again. Viagra failed, and when I proposed injections, Jill turned to Harold and said, "Dearest husband. I think I will like this treatment very much. I want you to try it."

"That's easy for you to say," responded Harold. "You're not the one who needs to stick a needle into your privates!"

"Oh, come on, Braveheart. Let's give it a try." They did, and with much success too, according to the reports I received from Jill. Better yet, Harold's own erections began to return after a few months, and Viagra worked for the first time. Before too long,

Harold used Viagra only for "special occasions," because his own erections were usually fine.

When Harold and Jill returned for a follow-up visit six months afterward, I asked Jill what it had been like for *her* to have experienced all these different treatments and their effects on their sex life together.

"It was all quite odd, to tell the truth," she replied thoughtfully. "Never-ending erections with injections, planning sex around meals with Viagra. It was all so different from how things were before the surgery. But we adjusted, we made jokes, and we ended up having fun with all of it. If you really think about it, there's nothing so 'normal' about sex anyway. The trick for me was to be able to give up the idea that sex is supposed to follow some predetermined script."

I thought there was wisdom in what Jill said, not only with regard to sex, but to the rest of life, and to relationships as well.

Learning from Viagra

Prostate cancer treatment poses a set of unusual sexual challenges to men and their partners. For men undergoing surgery, the change is abrupt, and particularly for men who know that their nerves will not be saved, they can be facing the knowledge that the last sex they will ever be able to have without assistance might be the night before surgery.

Other sexual changes faced by men undergoing radical prostatectomy include a lack of ejaculation: no fluid comes out when they have an orgasm. Everything that makes the fluid has been removed or tied off at surgery. Surprisingly, this does not seem to interfere with the pleasurable feeling of orgasm. Most men don't notice much difference. Some men even say the feeling is more intense after surgery.

It surprises many men to discover they can still have an orgasm, albeit a dry one, after their prostate cancer surgery. Prostate cancer treatment, including surgery, does not mean the end of a man's sex life. Surgery does not harm the nerves that provide sexual feeling to the penis or the nerves involved in achieving an orgasm. Amazingly, even men who can't achieve an erection can still almost always have an orgasm. It may simply take more effort with a soft penis.

Facing impotence brings up a variety of emotional issues for men. Foremost among these, in my experience, is the sense of mortality and of becoming instantly "old." Whereas most men who develop erectile dysfunction see the problem developing gradually, and often over years, men facing prostate cancer treatment experience the change immediately. Moreover, many of the men undergoing surgery for prostate cancer are in excellent health, whereas men with erectile dysfunction usually have some medical condition that has contributed to the dysfunction.

It is remarkable how important the ability to have sex can be for men, and this becomes evident as men face treatment for prostate cancer. The emotional impact of surgery or radiation seems not as great for men who already have developed impotence. But for men facing the prospect of suddenly losing the ability to "perform" sexually brings up issues of becoming instantly old, of loneliness, and of fear of never being loved again.

It is no mere accident that the word *impotent* connotes both erectile dysfunction as well as powerlessness. I see the feeling of powerlessness every week in men who have lost their erections as a result of prostate cancer treatment. These men walk differently, they talk differently, and it is obvious that they experience themselves differently. It is almost as if they feel they have been taken out of the world they lived in previously. Restoring erections in these men provides more than just a firm penis. It is also a treatment for the soul.

Women find it difficult to know exactly how to behave when their partner faces choices about prostate cancer treatments that may render him impotent. It is difficult to balance the desire to be supportive and accepting with one's own feelings and wishes. There is no right answer as to how to act. However, as Jill pointed out, it is easier to adapt to new situations and to be able to still enjoy one another if one can give up the notion that life, or sex, is supposed to be a certain way.

Viagra remains the first-line therapy for any man with erection problems after prostate cancer treatment, yet its effectiveness may be disappointing, particularly for men after radical prostatectomy in which the nerves have been injured. Viagra works best in these men if they are already able to have partial erections, and then the medication can give them the necessary boost.

Lessons

- All prostate cancer treatments, with external beam radiation, radioactive seeds, or surgery, can cause trouble for erections.

- Surgery can cause additional sexual changes, including loss of ejaculatory fluid. Sensation in the penis is unchanged, however, and the vast majority of men can still have an orgasm, even if the penis never becomes firm.

- Viagra is the most commonly prescribed therapy for men after prostate cancer treatment, but it is frequently ineffective in these men, particularly after surgery. The best results are seen in men who have had nerve sparing on both sides, with less effectiveness in men with only one spared nerve. Viagra does not work at all for men when neither of the paired nerves has been spared, since Viagra acts by enhancing the nerve signal. No nerve means no signal, and no signal means that Viagra has nothing to enhance.

- There are other options available besides Viagra to help men have satisfying sexual relations after prostate cancer treatment. Penile injections are highly effective without requiring the presence of intact nerves. Other choices are penile implants, vacuum devices, or a pellet placed in the opening of the penis that mimics the action of the penile injections.

- Some men who know that they will be impotent after cancer surgery may choose to have an implant placed at the same operation.

- Psychologically, prostate cancer treatment can be difficult for men because they must deal with issues related to mortality and aging, in addition to concerns about their sexuality.

- Men who are not in stable, long-term relationships may face the most difficult decisions and stresses, since they may see successful sexuality as a necessary step in finding and then keeping a partner.

- Women struggle too as their partners deal with prostate cancer and the consequences of treatment. Although safety and effective treatment of the cancer are the most critical issues, sexuality may be of great importance as well. The more involved the woman can be in pretreatment and posttreatment medical decisions, the better it will be for the relationship, sexually and otherwise.

- Women have a range of reactions to prostate cancer treatments that may render their partners impotent. For women who do not find sex pleasurable, it may actually be a relief to consider a future without sexual contact. For others who do enjoy physical intimacy, the changes that occur with cancer treatment can cause a sense of loss, sadness, and loneliness.

- Successful emotional adjustment following cancer treatment requires an ability to adjust to new circumstances and a willingness to try new things. Relationships flourish when both partners can accept what life brings them for themselves and for each other.

Frequently Asked Questions About Viagra

Q: How effective is Viagra for erectile dysfunction?

A: Viagra works in about 80 percent of men with performance anxiety and in about two-thirds of men with other types of erectile dysfunction. It cannot, however, solve potency problems related to emotional or relationship problems.

Q: Is there anything like Viagra for women?

A: Not yet. But there is much ongoing interest in finding ways to help women who have low desire, difficulty achieving orgasm, painful intercourse, or inadequate lubrication.

Q: How well does Viagra work for men after surgery for prostate cancer?

A: Not so well. It's worth a try, but at best only half of these men will be satisfied with Viagra.

Q: Are there other treatments for erectile dysfunction if Viagra doesn't work?

A: Yes! Among the other effective treatments are injections, external vacuum devices, penile implants, and even hormone treatments for some men. Men who fail Viagra should seek treatment from a specialist in the field, usually a urologist.

Q: Is Viagra dangerous?

A: No. Viagra is remarkably safe.

Q: What about all the stories that Viagra causes heart attacks and deaths?

A: There was considerable misinformation about this when Viagra first became available, and the media scared a lot of people with their stories. Viagra has now been extensively studied, and there is no evidence whatsoever that Viagra is bad for the heart or that it causes heart attacks or deaths.

Q: Is there anyone who should *not* take Viagra?

A: Men who take nitrate medication for the heart should never take Viagra. This includes men who have been prescribed nitroglycerin but don't use it much. Nitrates taken together with Viagra can severely lower the blood pressure. Men with heart disease who do *not* take nitrates can take Viagra safely.

Q: Are nitrites a problem?

A: Nitrites are different from nitrates and are perfectly safe. They are found in many smoked foods, such as hot dogs, salami, and smoked turkey. They have no interaction with Viagra.

Q: My doctor prescribed nitroglycerin for me a few years ago in case I get chest pain, but I've never used it. Can I take Viagra anyway?

A: I strongly recommend against it. Sexual activity might cause you to have chest pain, and you will then be strongly tempted to take your nitroglycerin. If you really never use the nitroglycerin, ask your doctor whether you still need it. If your doctor gives you permission to throw it away, you can then safely use Viagra.

Q: What are the side effects I might experience taking Viagra?

A: Viagra side effects can be annoying, but none is dangerous. The most common are headache, stuffy nose, flushing of the face, and upset stomach. About 3 percent of men notice a blue haze for a few hours.

Q: What if Viagra doesn't work?

A: It is important to remember that there are other effective treatments available. As my colleague says, "If you own a penis, we can give you an erection." Go see a specialist in sexual dysfunction, which is usually a urologist.

Q: Why didn't Viagra work for me?

A: The usual reasons are that the medication just isn't strong enough to overcome the problem, or it wasn't taken properly, or your problem is psychological.

Q: How can Viagra be taken improperly?

A: There are four common mistakes.

1. The dosage is too low. Many men require the full dose of 100 milligrams in order to see any significant benefit.

2. Having sex too soon after taking the drug. Viagra takes a while to be absorbed. Peak levels occur after one hour if taken on an empty stomach and longer if taken with food. If you try to have sex too soon, you may be missing out on the best chance for Viagra to help.

3. Taking Viagra with food. Absorption is delayed if Viagra is taken with food or alcohol in the stomach.

4. Didn't actually try to have sex. Viagra does not *create* an erection by itself. It just *helps* the erection if a person is sexually stimulated or aroused.

Q: My partner and I usually have sex in the evening, after dinner. What can I do to avoid the delayed absorption of Viagra with food in my stomach?

A: Take Viagra thirty minutes or so *before* the meal. The beneficial effects of Viagra usually last for four to eight hours afterward.

Q: What does Viagra do to a man with a normal erection?

A: Many men have no noticeable change. But some find that the penis is indeed harder, and others will be able to achieve a second or even third erection more easily after orgasm.

Q: What happens to women who take Viagra?

A: So far, the studies have not shown much benefit for women. However, some women with poor blood flow to the vagina, because of pelvic surgery or radiation, may lubricate better by taking Viagra, which may make sex more pleasurable.

Q: How do the new erection pills compare to Viagra?

A: It's too soon to tell.

Q: How long does Viagra work?

A: About four to eight hours for most men.

Q: How far ahead of intercourse should I take Viagra?

A: Some men have benefit as early as twenty minutes after taking Viagra, but the optimal effect usually occurs at one hour.

Q: Is Viagra only for older men?

A: Viagra is a good treatment for men of any age who are having difficulties with erections.

Q: My wife and I are struggling a lot, and our sex life has gone downhill. Will Viagra help?

A: Viagra helps blood flow to the penis. It is not a solution for relationship issues, unless those problems stem directly from a sexual problem.

Q: Is Viagra useful for young men whose impotence is due to anxiety?

A: Yes.

Q: Is it dishonest to take Viagra?

A: Not at all. But the more important and serious the relationship, the more important it is to be open and honest, including being truthful about medications or other things that influence "performance."

Q: If I am just dating casually, should I tell my partner I'm taking Viagra?

A: I don't believe you have to reveal everything about yourself to someone you've only recently met. However, I would strongly urge any man to tell his partner about Viagra use as early as possible in a developing relationship.

Q: Will Viagra increase my sexual desire?

A: Not directly. Viagra works on the penis, not the brain. But many men do find themselves more interested in sex if their erections are better and more reliable, and Viagra may therefore increase libido in this way.

Q: How can sex be spontaneous if I have to plan ahead with Viagra?

A: Spontaneity is a problem for men with erectile dysfunction, and Viagra doesn't really solve this problem very well. But many men do respond within twenty minutes if Viagra is taken on an empty stomach, and there is no reason that foreplay can't fill that time. Research is being done to find ways to make these types of medications act more quickly. For now, penile injection therapy or a penile prosthesis may be a better treatment choice if more spontaneity is desired.

Q: Will Viagra make me want to have sex with everyone?

A: Only if you already want to have sex with everyone.

Q: Will my husband start chasing after younger women if he
starts taking Viagra?

A: Only if he already wants to be chasing after younger women.

Q: Is Viagra an aphrodisiac?

A: No.

Q: Will my partner feel differently about me if I take Viagra?

A: Viagra can often restore the sex life for a couple who has
stopped having sex because of impotence and can thus bring
back physical intimacy to a relationship. This is almost always
very positive.

Q: What if I don't have a problem with erections and take Viagra
only to improve my sexual performance? Will my lover feel
differently about me if she discovers I take Viagra?

A: The risk of secretly taking Viagra is that your partner may fear
you are being dishonest with her in other ways too. For this
reason, it is best to tell your partner about Viagra use as early
as possible.

Q: Does Viagra ever help relationships?

A: Definitely. Sexual problems can create stress in relationships,
and this may be greatly improved with Viagra in many cases.
This in turn may help some couples be able to enjoy each
other more.

Q: Can a man be too old to take Viagra?

A: Can a woman be too old to buy shoes?

Q: Is there any way to avoid the headaches that I get with
Viagra?

A: Headaches can often be avoided by taking the usual treatments, such as aspirin, acetaminophen, or ibuprofen, either
just before or at the same time as Viagra.

Q: How often can I safely take Viagra?
A: Once a day.

Q: Will Viagra become less effective if I take it often?
A: No.

Q: Will I become dependent on Viagra if my own erections were okay to begin with?
A: Not physically. But some men may feel that they are adequate lovers only if their penis has the extra firmness they get by using Viagra, and they may then be reluctant to stop taking it.

Q: Will Viagra make me gain weight?
A: No.

Q: Will Viagra make me more attractive?
A: No.

Q: Can a woman tell if I've taken Viagra?
A: A woman who has read this book might be suspicious if your face and ears become bright red and you complain about your headache, stuffy nose, and the blue haze you see around lights. Otherwise, there's no way for her to tell.

Q: Do older women resent it when their husbands take Viagra?
A: Some older women have never learned to enjoy sex or have medical conditions that make intercourse unpleasant. These women are often relieved when their husbands develop impotence, and they may be unhappy if Viagra rekindles sexual interest in their mates. But many women of any age will be thrilled to be able to enjoy a physical relationship with their partners once again.

Q: Can anything bad happen if I stop taking Viagra?
A: No.

Q: Will my partner think I'm a jerk or a nerd because I need to take Viagra?

A: Most women will happily accept a man they truly care for, regardless of his human frailties. Being open about one's need for Viagra should not be a problem if there exists a bond of warmth and affection. But women don't like to feel duped and are likely to think poorly of a man whom they have discovered is taking Viagra secretly in order to impress them.

Q: Will I be able to have sex all night if I take Viagra?

A: Guys who can't climb a flight of stairs without huffing and puffing shouldn't expect to be able to have an all-night sex romp, even with Viagra. The heart and lungs will quit long before the penis does. If marathon sex is the goal, I recommend aerobic exercise training.

Q: What can we learn from Viagra?

A: Viagra has provided us with a window with which to see the wonderfully complex nature of sexuality and human relationships. As a medication, it has proved highly effective at restoring sexual function to many men with a physical cause for their erectile dysfunction and has even proven to be an enormous boon for men who suffer from performance anxiety.

Somewhere along the way, though, we have latched onto Viagra as if it were a cure for whatever has failed us in ourselves and in our relationships. So many men have taken Viagra in the hopes of solving deep-seated psychological problems or sticky relationship conflicts, only to be sorely disappointed. This is the Viagra Myth.

The answers to our most difficult life problems cannot be provided by a little blue pill, no matter how powerful the medication. The path to personal growth almost always requires hard work, in the form of self-examination, honest communication, and acceptance of oneself and others. It is inspiring to be a witness to that kind of growth. Yet thanks to my patients, I find myself inspired almost every single day.

Epilogue: The Future
of the Viagra Myth

When I started working in the field of sexual dysfunction, I didn't know that I would become privy to such a wide range of emotions and expectations among my patients. I was trained as a surgeon, after all, and although I had enjoyed my rotation through psychiatry during medical school, little did I know that the most fascinating part of my daily work life would be learning about the personal struggles of the men and their partners who came to me for help. With expertise on the anatomy of the penis, of all things, I came full circle to the intricacies of the mind. To think of sex as merely blood flow to the penis is to lose sight of the incredible panorama of human relationships, and I am reminded of this every day by the men and women who come through my office door.

In these pages I have shared some of the stories of my patients as they have struggled with concerns about their sexual function, relationship issues, and their own personal fears. All too often, these men have sought the solution to their life issues by turning to the little blue pill that has captured our imagination, the pill with a name that suggests vigor and vitality combined with the power of Niagara Falls.

In a world of convenience, of drive-through fast food, cell phones, instant messaging, and global positioning systems in our automobiles, it is no wonder that we look for the quick and easy fix even when it comes to our personal lives. Deified in our popular culture, Viagra has become the single solution to all our sexual, personal, and relationship issues:

"I'm too nervous to get an erection when I first meet someone."
"Take Viagra."

"My erection isn't firm enough."
"Take Viagra."

"I ejaculate too quickly."
"Take Viagra."

"I've lost the feeling for my girlfriend."
"Take Viagra."

"I want to feel like a superstud."
"Take Viagra."

"I want my new partner to fall in love with me."
"Take Viagra."

To borrow and update an old phrase, if Viagra didn't exist, we would have to invent it. Together with its remarkable ability to improve blood flow to the erectile chambers of the penis, we have also imbued the little blue pill with an almost magical ability to solve our most difficult relationship issues.

As we've seen in the previous chapters, Viagra can indeed work wonders for men with erection problems. And if there are relationship or personal issues that stem directly from the inability to achieve an adequate erection, then Viagra may work minor miracles.

Viagra is safe, easily available, and promoted by U.S. senators and high-profile athletes. It is no wonder that the Viagra Myth arose.

Yet complex or deeply rooted issues can never be successfully treated by Viagra, because a pill cannot change the essence of who we are or how we relate to others. But this doesn't stop men from trying Viagra. It's so much easier than looking inside oneself or, heaven forbid, having an honest conversation with one's partner.

And yet as much as we look to easy solutions, we also distrust things that do not seem natural, including medications. We search out organic food, drink certified-pure spring water, eat free-range chicken, and fear antibiotics and environmental estrogens in our food supply. We treat high-voltage power lines and computer monitors with caution. When we place this distrust of all things artificial next to the American tradition of toughing it out against life's hardest problems and adding a dash of residual puritanism that permeates our culture, there is a tension in our world regarding the use of a medication to enhance our sexual lives.

As if to illustrate this, just recently a prominent local celebrity of an intellectual bent returned to see me in follow-up. I had treated him for a minor urinary infection, and at the time I inquired whether he was having any sexual problems he wished to discuss with me. He was a healthy man in his early fifties, handsome in a boyish way, who was happily married with two teenage children. As it turned out, he had struggled with premature ejaculation his entire life, and I eventually offered him a Viagra six-pack to see if it would help.

After he related today that his infection symptoms had disappeared, I asked him whether he had tried the Viagra. His face lit up with an impish smile. "Yup," he said. "It worked really well. I tried it only twice, but my wife was very pleased both times."

"What about you? Were you pleased?"

"Sure I was. But the Viagra had been a hard sell for my wife, so the fact that it worked out was great. When I first told her you'd given me Viagra, she was upset that I would even consider taking it. She's the kind of woman who might occasionally take an aspirin for a headache, but that's all. She won't even take a decongestant if she has a bad cold because she doesn't like putting anything that isn't natural into her body. 'I'm surprised you would take a strong drug like Viagra just to help with sex,' she said to me."

"So what happened?" I asked.

"I told her what you had told me. That Viagra was a safe medication, and why shouldn't I try something that might make me feel better about myself sexually? I think she was also reassured that you hadn't given me a prescription, but only a supply of six pills. How much trouble could six pills cause? It turned out to be the best sex we've had in years, both times I used it," he said with obvious satisfaction.

"Well, I'm glad Viagra worked so well for you. Now that you know it's effective, would you like me to write a prescription for you?"

"No thanks," he said. "Let me see how it goes the next few times. I confess that I share some of my wife's attitudes. We both have a tendency to think poorly of people who resort to medications in order to get through life's tough patches. I'm not convinced that I need a pill to help me with my sexual relationship with my wife, even though the experience was interesting, to say the least. I'll give you a call if I change my mind about that Viagra prescription."

This is the counterpoint to the Viagra Myth. Even when a pill brings about pleasure, satisfaction, and an improved sense of well-being, we hold back from wholly embracing it. Perhaps this is the reason that only 50 percent of new Viagra prescriptions are refilled in the United States. We want the results, yet we feel guilty about it at the same time. "Yes, it felt good, but isn't it wrong for me to use a medicine for sex?"

What does the future hold? Within the next few years, there will almost certainly be a host of new medications and treatments to aid sexuality and to enhance it, for both men and women. Already there are two major competitors of Viagra on the market in Europe, and it is expected that they will both be approved for use in the United States by the end of 2003. One of these, Cialis, has the promising feature of lasting as long as thirty-six to forty-eight hours. This means you could take a single pill on Friday night and be a star all weekend. The claim regarding the other, Levitra, is that it begins working as soon as fifteen minutes after swallowing it, allowing for greater sexual spontaneity than with Viagra. A nose spray is being developed that will allow the entry of sexually enhancing medications into the bloodstream within seconds.

Other treatments for men include creams to apply to the penis, more potent suppositories to be placed inside the urethra, and pills to help control ejaculation more effectively. For women, there will also be pills, creams, and gadgets. Already, there is a miniature suction cup device on the market that is placed on the clitoris to help stimulate swelling, increased sensitivity, and vaginal lubrication. More treatments and pills, some with effects that we cannot even yet imagine, are sure to come our way within the next ten years.

What will we do with all these treatments? We will use them. We will experiment with them and laugh about it all with our partners. Or we may keep our use of these new treatments secret from our partners and hope that our appeal as a sexual being has been enhanced.

Yet no matter how much technology and pharmacology advance, there are core issues for all of us that will undoubtedly remain: Am I lovable? Am I attractive? Can anyone accept me for who I am? Will I always be alone? Is it normal to want sex this much? Is there something wrong with me? Why do I feel so different from everyone else? and Will I ever find true love?

In this age of fast-moving people and stressful lifestyles, so many of us lead an isolated existence where these questions reverberate without answer. Even amid a stable home, loving family, and close community, these core issues regularly arise. In a fragmented society of lonely individuals, these questions can become larger than life. As long as they exist, there will always be a premium on sexual performance as a surrogate for finding love and acceptance among others and in oneself. There will always be a search for a magic, easy solution to our most difficult and vexing problems. Long after Viagra has been supplanted by more effective medications and even when Viagra becomes no more than a historical footnote, there will always be the Viagra Myth.

Further Reading

Books

Altman, Alan M. M., and Laurie Ashner. *Making Love the Way We Used to . . . or Better: Secrets to Satisfying Midlife Sexuality*. New York: McGraw-Hill, 2002.

Berman, J., L. Berman, and E. Bumiller. *For Women Only: A Revolutionary Guide to Overcoming Sexual Dysfunction and Reclaiming Your Sex Life*. New York: Henry Holt, 2001.

Chesler, Phyllis. *About Men*. Orlando: Harcourt, 1990.

Farrell, Warren. *Why Men Are the Way They Are*. New York: Berkley Publishing Group, 1990.

Fowers, Blaine. *Beyond the Myth of Marital Happiness: How Embracing the Virtues of Loyalty, Generosity, Justice, and Courage Can Strengthen Your Relationship*. San Francisco: Jossey-Bass, 2000.

Gurian, Michael. *The Wonder of Boys: What Parents, Mentors, and Educators Can Do to Shape Boys into Exceptional Men*. Los Angeles: J. P. Tarcher, 1997.

Kantoff, Philip, and Malcom McConnell. *Prostate Cancer: A Family Consultation with Dr. Philip Kantoff*. Boston: Houghton Mifflin, 1996.

Kipnis, Aaron R. *Knights Without Armor: A Practical Guide for Men in Quest of Masculine Soul*. New York: J. P. Tarcher, 1991.

Morgentaler, Abraham. *The Male Body: A Physician's Guide to What Every Man Should Know About His Sexual Health*. New York: Fireside/Simon and Schuster, 1993.

Zilbergeld, Bernie. *The New Male Sexuality*. New York: Bantam Doubleday Dell, 1999.

Articles

Barnard, A. "Men Seek the Truth on Prostate Treatments," *Boston Globe*, Jan. 18, 2003, p. A1.

Brindley, Giles. "Cavernosal Alpha-Blockade: A New Technique for Investigating and Treating Erectile Dysfunction." *British Journal of Psychiatry*, 1983, *143*, 332–337.

Goldstein, I., T. F. Lue, H. Padma-Nathan, R. C. Rosen, W. D. Steers, and P. A. Wicker. "Oral Sildenafil in the Treatment of Erectile Dysfunction." *New England Journal of Medicine*, 1998, *338*, 1397–1404.

Khoudary, K., W. C. DeWolf, C. O. Bruning III, and A. Morgentaler. "Immediate Sexual Rehabilitation in Radical Prostatectomy Patients by Simultaneous Placement of Penile Prosthesis: Initial Results in Fifty Patients." *Urology*, 1997, *50*, 395–399.

Laumann, E. O., A. Paik, and R. C. Rosen. "Sexual Dysfunction in the United States: Prevalence and Predictors." *Journal of the American Medical Association*, 1999, *281*, 537–544.

Morgentaler, Abraham. "Male Impotence," *Lancet*, 1999, *354*, 1713–1718.

NIH Consensus Development Panel on Impotence. *Journal of the American Medical Association*, 1998, *270*, 83–90.

About the Author

Abraham Morgentaler, M.D., F.A.C.S., is an associate clinical professor at Harvard Medical School and an internationally recognized expert on sexuality and male reproduction. In 1999, Dr. Morgentaler founded a unique center devoted to sexual and reproductive issues for men called Men's Health Boston. Dr. Morgentaler is a recipient of the prestigious New Investigator Award granted by the American Foundation of Urological Disease and is the author of *The Male Body: A Physician's Guide to What Every Man Should Know About His Sexual Health*. Dr. Morgentaler lectures around the world on sexuality, his extensive research has appeared in prominent medical journals such as *The New England Journal of Medicine*, *The Lancet*, and *The Journal of the American Medical Association*, and he has appeared on the NBC *Nightly News* with Tom Brokaw, CBS's *The Early Show*, and NPR radio.

A native of Montreal, Canada, Dr. Morgentaler now lives in the Boston area with his two daughters.